A VIEW FROM THE TOWER

Stories of Old Wallasey

P. Davies

Dedicated to my friends and family

CONTENTS

Title Page
Dedication
Chapter Images
The Tallest Tower ... 1
When War Came To Wallasey ... 11
When The Law Prohibited Bathing ... 20
Old Cottages, Manors And Quiet Corners ... 24
New Brighton Lifeboat ... 28
Market Gardening In Wallasey ... 31
The Wallasey Frog Man ... 33
Wallasey and the Great War ... 35
The New Brighton Open Air Bathing Pool ... 38
The Dark Town Brigade ... 43
Progress That Swept Away old Wallasey ... 48
Wallasey In The 1920's ... 54
Battle of the Brickworks ... 58
The Hermit of Wallasey ... 64
The House in the Park ... 67
Egremont ... 71
In and Around Egremont: Pictorial ... 75
Snow Balling at Seacombe ... 85

Winston in Wallasey	87
Wallasey Smithies	89
The Sexton and the Fire	92
Wallasey Village	95
In And Around Wallasey Village in The 1950's: Pictorial	98
Cymbals at the Council	108
Joggers, Trams and Buses	111
Shanty Town	115
Wallasey Cricket Club	117
Wallasey In The 1930's	120
Wallasey Ferryboats That Sailed Off To War	128
Liscard & The Monkey House	136
Shopping In Liscard: Pictorial	142
Last Orders Please!	151
Days of Outings and Celebration	158
The Potter of Seacombe	161
Tombstones of the Past	164
The 'Gem' Disaster	167
The Promenade	171
Promenade Construction: Pictorial	173
Stormy Weather	177
First Wallasey Baths?	180
In and Around Old Wallasey	181
Ivy Wallasey	189
The Wallasey Wreckers	191
Old Court Yard	197
Naming Your Street	199
Wallasey In The 1940's	207

Wallasey's World Famous Farm	214
The Beginnings Of Wallasey Football	217
When Poulton Was Famous For its Trees	222
The School Born On A Ferryboat	228
Wallasey at the Pictures	231
The Devil's Nest	235
The Ham And Egg Parade	236
Days of Dole and Struggle	239
The Sights And Sounds Of The Little Streets	244
The Heroes Of The Wallasey A.R.P	247
Acknowledgement	253

CHAPTER IMAGES

The Tallest Tower - New Brighton Promenade, 1914
When War Came To Wallasey - Wheatland Lane bomb damage, 1940
When The Law Prohibited Bathing - New Brighton shore with bathing machines, c1900
Old Cottages, Manors And Quiet Corners - View of Oxton Road, 1924
New Brighton Lifeboat 1860s-1960s - The lifeboat 'Rescue'
Market Gardening In Wallasey - View of Wallasey Village allotments
The Wallasey Frog Man - British midget submarine
Wallasey and the Great War - Construction begins on the Town Hall, 1914
The New Brighton Opening Air Bathing Pool - The frontage of the Open Air Bathing Pool
The Dark Town Brigade - Wallasey Fire Station, Liscard Village
Progress That Swept Away Old Wallasey - Mona Cottage, Liscard Village
Wallasey in the 1920's - View of Grove Road and Hose Side Road, c1920
Battle of the Brickworks - Egremont Beach, 1912
The Hermit of Wallasey - Funeral cortege of Frederick Krueger, 1909
The House In The Park - Liscard Hall, 1926
Egremont - View of Egremont from the Pier, c1912
In and Around Egremont: Pictorial - Davey Jones Locker, Egremont
Snow Balling at Seacombe - Borough Road, 1904

Winston in Wallasey - Winston Churchill near Dock Road, April 1941

Wallasey Smithies - View of a blacksmith at work, Liscard Village, c1912

Sexton and the Fire - Sketch of St. Hilary's Church, c1850

Wallasey Village - Early view of Wallasey Mill high on the Breck

In And Around Wallasey Village In The 1950's : Pictorial - Queen Elizabeth II at Grove Road Station on her visit to Wallasey

Cymbals at the Council - Former Council offices, corner of Church Street and King Street

Joggers, Trams and Buses - Milnes double-decker horse tramway, 1893

Shanty Town - Flooded out in Moreton, c1914

Wallasey Cricket Club - Modern view of the Club House

Wallasey in the 1930's - Derby Pool bathing belles, 1932

Wallasey Ferryboats That Sailed Off To War - Iris and Daffodil at anchor with a tug after their return from naval service in 1918

Liscard & The Monkey House - Monkey House, Liscard

Shopping In Liscard: Pictorial - View of Liscard, 1980

Last Orders Please! - Coach & Horses, Moreton, c1910

Days of Outings and Celebration - Moreton carnival, Hoylake Road, 1920s

The Potter of Seacombe - view of the Seacombe Pottery, 1889

Tombstones of the Past - St. Hilary's Church and Tower

The 'Gem' Disaster - Sketch of the 'Gem' ferryboat

The Promenade - View of a completed part of the Promenade, 1912

Promenade Construction: Pictorial - The extent of the Promanade to the Red Noses, 1932

Stormy Weather - Storm damage at Open Air Bsthing Pool which was flooded in March, 1990

First Wallasey Baths - Seacombe Ferry, c1876

In And Around Old Wallasey - Poulton Road crossroad of Mill Lane & Breck Road, c1900

Ivy Wallasey - Magazine Brow Mersey Cottages, c1912
The Wallasey Wreckers - Painting by Hobbs of Mother Redcap's, 1888
Old Court Yard - Oakdale Court Yard, Seacombe, 1905
Naming Your Street - Claremount Road, with Rosclare Drive on the left, 1927
Wallasey in the 1940's - Marks & Spencers, Liscard, bomb damage, March 1941
Wallasey's Most Famous Farm - view of the Model Farm buildings, 1907
The Beginnings of Wallasey Football - Rakers at New Brighton Tower Ground, 1966
When Poulton Was Famous For Its Trees - Poulton Bridge Road, 1912
The School Born On A Ferryboat - Wallasey High School, 1909
Wallasey at the Pictures - Animated Pictures, 1906
The Devil's Nest - View of the small properties, c1850
The Ham And Egg Parade - View of the Ham & Egg Parade, 1890's
The Days of Dole and Struggle - Seacombe Ferry during General Strike with mesh on bus windows, May 1926
Sights And Sounds of the Little Streets - Seaview Road, 1910
The Heroes of the Wallasey A.R.P - Stroudes Corner, Rake Lane, bomb damage, 1940

THE TALLEST TOWER

As the title of the book suggests, many years ago you could view Wallasey from a tall tower. A 621 foot landmark in steel that stood high in New Brighton. It was bigger than Blackpool's. A sort of answer in its time to the Eiffel Tower in Paris. The town was proud of it. Everybody talked about it. It cost £120,000 – and seven lives – to build. It was the tallest structure in the United Kingdom. It only lasted nineteen years. The big, bold enterprise never paid.

Just over a century ago the last of the tower fell to the ground. It had been a big, brave gamble that didn't pay off.

New Brighton Tower views from postcards, c1905

A VIEW FROM THE TOWER

Wallasey Road with Moseley Avenue left, c1930s.

It was on a July day in 1896 that plans for it were announced. The town buzzed with the news.

The New Brighton Tower and Recreation Company Limited (share capital, £300,000) was born. It bought the 20-acre site adjacent the promenade and called it The Tower Grounds.

"It is intended," said the company, "to erect on a portion of the site a tower, with assembly hall, winter garden, a restaurant and refreshment rooms." The rest of the site was to be laid out as a pleasure ground.

"The well known architects, Messrs. Maxwell and Tuke, of Manchester, who designed and superintended the construction of the Blackpool tower, have been engaged for the past eleven months upon the designs," continued the company statement.

The architects were quoted as saying that the tower would be built of mild steel, would be octagonal in plan, and would have a width at the ground line of 135 feet, and a height above the ground line of 544 feet, or 47 feet higher than Blackpool's tower.

Building started in 1897. On 13th January two men lost their lives and a third was seriously injured. An iron girder had been hoisted 50 feet when the hook of the crane snapped.

In April of the same year another man died during construction operations. By this time the tower had reached a height of 180 feet.

Early in June came another tragedy. A labourer fell to his death down a lift-hole to the base of the structure.

Letters started to appear in the newspapers, calling for safety nets to be set up round the building. "The risk to human life increases every day," wrote one correspondent.

In August, 1897, the newspapers reported "Another Fatality at the Tower Grounds". A workman fell 100 feet.

In September came the sixth fatality. A man fell 60 feet. There were more letters in the papers about the "mounting dangers".

The Tower Grounds were opened at Whitsun, 1897. They were incomplete, but sufficiently advanced to draw great crowds.

It was the following year that the Tower itself was completed and opened to the public. It was described as "the highest structure in the United Kingdom".

A few days before the opening tragedy had struck again. The Tower had been threatened by fire, and a young member of the volunteer Seacombe Fire Brigade perished in a 90-foot fall while fighting the flames.

The finished structure stood 621 feet above the level of the old dock sill in Liverpool. It tapered to a height of nearly 500 feet above the brickwork erected at the base.

An army of 3,500 workmen had been engaged day and night to get the Tower ready for the Whit Monday opening.

There were four lifts. Trips to the top cost sixpence. It was quite some ride.

Of the view from the top, the 'Wallasey News' said: "All the Wirral Peninsula can be seen, and the Great Orme's Head, and part of the Lake District."

The theatre underneath it, with seating for 3,500 people, was reported to have the largest stage of any theatre in the world. Prices ranged from sixpence for 'the gods' to one guinea for the grandeur of a box.

The theatre quickly established a reputation for staging the spectacular. It bought big-scale epics – Samuel F. Cody's Wild West show "The Klondyke Nugget" (complete with snowstorm), Colonel-Brown's 'Wild West Show', with 'real redskins and genuine cowboys'.

In the early years of the last century Sunday concerts really put the theatre on the map. Most of the great artistes of the time appeared there – Irish tenor singer John McCormack, Italian female operatic singer Luisa Tetrazzini, Dame Clara Butt and Dame Nellie Melba, also operatic singers.

World's greatest violin master, Fritz Kreisler, came in 1910. Sir Edward Elgar, composer, was there on 4th July, 1899, to attend the first performance of his 'Minuet'.

The Tower Ballroom

The distinguished classical dancer Maud Allen appeared in August of that year, and created a mild sensation with her 'impressionistic mood settings' dance routines. The theatre was packed, and many members of the audience were reported as 'openly expressing disapproval'. Miss Allan had to appeal for silence.
Variety shows starred Harry Lauder, Harry Tate, Charles Coburn ('The Man Who Broke the Bank at Monte Carlo'), Vesta Tilley, Duggie Wakefield and Gracie Fields – 'By Request' in 1925.
The Tower Grounds drew vast crowds in the last years of the nineteenth century and the first years of the last. They were rightly named 'a mecca for the North'.
In November 1898, the Tower had its first suicide leap. A young man threw himself from the balcony outside it.
At the annual general meeting of the Tower Company in Decem-

ber, 1898, it was reported that despite all the delays and setbacks, including "the very indifferent steamboat service provided by Wallasey Urban District Council", nearly half a million people had visited the Tower during the year.

Demolition of the Tower, 1919

From the top of the Tower, the panoramic view into the years looked good, but the period of prosperity for the venture was in fact to be very brief.

The coming of World War One marked the beginning of the end. Business slackened. The crowds grew thinner. Owing to neglect during the war years, the structure became unsafe. The amount needed to renovate and maintain it became so great that its owners decided to dismantle it.

"The decision will be received with a certain sadness by the town," said the 'Wallasey News' at the time. "It has become a part of the place, a landmark for which many thousands of people, here and elsewhere, have a real affection."

Demolition was started in May, 1919. The last of the steel girders came tumbling down in June, 1921. Over 1,000 tons of steel were removed.

"The Tower," said the 'Wallasey News', "was the first sight to greet the eye of the stranger coming into the Mersey and the first to welcome home the traveller from Wallasey. The town has lost something splendid."

There was criticism of the Corporation. It was said – in the Council, in the press – that if the local authority had given the project more help and support the Tower might not have had to come down.

It was reported that in the nineteen years of the Tower's life the company had spent £40,000 advertising the attractions of New Brighton. Over the same period the Corporation had spent £1,000.

It was to have been a centre of pleasure and sport, a worthy rival to Blackpool. As it turned out, it was a damp squib. It fizzed, but never quite went off.

The theatre went up in flames in April 1969. There is no evidence left of the mighty enterprise that once stood proud in New Brighton.

NEW BRIGHTON *from the Air*

A VIEW FROM THE TOWER

Comparison Picture to Scale
New Brighton Tower 621 ft high
R.M.S. Lusitania and Mauretania 790 ft long

P. DAVIES

WHEN WAR CAME TO WALLASEY

The Wallasey Blitz was two years of death, danger and destruction. It was two years of heroism and courage. Streets were a mass of rubble and houses were ripped apart.

The blitz began with a 'false alarm' – the siren sounded for the first time on 25th June, 1940. It reached its awful peak during three nightmare days in March, 1941. It ended when the last bomb fell in January, 1942.

It took a total of 340 civilian lives. Over 270 people were seriously injured and 600 were hurt. The town heard 509 alerts. The 658 high explosives dropped on it demolished 1,150 houses and damaged 17,000.

The spirit and simple heroism of the warden and firemen in the streets and of the people in the shelters won through. The valour of the Wallasey A.R.P is covered in a later chapter.

It was on the evening of 10th August 1940 that sirens moaned out across Wallasey. Four people were killed when bombs fell in Seacombe, Poulton, Liscard and New Brighton. It was just a taste of the terror to come.

The Luftwaffe came back again on 30/31st August, when Wallasey received most of the bombs that fell on Merseyside. The south-western corner of the Town Hall received a direct hit. Seacombe suffered five nights later. Moreton came in for attention on 11th September.

More raids followed on 22nd, 26th and 29th September. In that month Wallasey was bombed a total of nine times. October was quiet (three raids). There were nine heavy raids in November.

On 6th November the King and Queen visited the town. They walked freely along the brick-scattered streets, chatting informally with the people. Wartime secrecy shrouded their visit, but the news spread like wildfire. Union Jacks flew from broken windows. In one of the town's largest air-raid shelters their Majesties were temporarily lost in the maze of passages. They were told that as many as 1,200 people had sheltered in it at one time. By the end of November, 1940, 19 people had been killed and 18 had been badly injured.

During the latter part of the month and most of December the enemy was not very active, but in the heavy raids of Christmas week Wallasey suffered severely.

Starting early in the evening of 20th December, the first raid lasted ten hours. The following night's attack lasted an hour longer than that.

German planes came over in waves as bombs fell continuously. The problem of housing and feeding the homeless was a heavy one. The Civil Defence workers tackled it heroically.

There were two nights of incessant bombardment. They were followed on 23rd December by raids made easy for the bombers by the great fires which blazed. Of Wallasey's 119 fatal casualties during the three nights, 13 were elderly inmates of a widows' home.

Compared with December, January and February of 1941 were

quiet. The worst raids of the war were to come in March. Whether by accident or design, the town shared with Birkenhead in that awful early Spring the brunt of a brutal attack.

The 12th, 13th and 14th were nights of fire and explosion and death. Incidents were so numerous that the Civil Defence were unable to reach an accurate total for their records. The raids were intense and casualties were heavy. The whole town was showered with incendiaries and high explosives. Rescue and demolition parties went sleepless, recovering the dead and the living. Fires raged about them. The grimmest moment during the attacks came when the water supply for fire-fighting failed.

Church Street suffered badly as the attacks continued. There was not reprieve. The Victoria Central Hospital, which stood in Liscard Road at that time, had to be evacuated owing to a breakdown in gas, water and electricity supplies.

The town was on the brink of evacuation as the effect of the raids was rendering large areas as uninhabitable. Almost all the services were put out of action by the relentless pounding by the Luftwaffe. Rest centres were established for the 10,000 homeless.

Wallasey endured so much during that month. Over 170 people had been killed and 158 seriously injured. Mr. Herbert Morrison, Home Secretary, said of the Civil Defence, "They are an example to the whole country."

One of the strangest stories to come from the horror of the March blitz was the discovery of a small survivor. When Lancaster Avenue and Wimbledon Street were bombed in the early morning of 12th March, thirty people were killed, most of them in a communal shelter. After three days the rescue party almost gave up of any hope in finding any more survivors until someone heard the faint cry of a baby. With the greatest of care the four month girl was unearthed from the rubble where she was only slightly hurt. Sadly her parents had been killed, their bodies protecting her from harm.

The following month was quiet. Three or four raids and no casualties. May brought heavy damage to the Liverpool docks and a large number of misaimed bombs hit Wallasey, killing three people and seriously injuring 19. One of the casualties was the ferryboat, 'Royal Daffodil', which was bombed and sunk at her moorings at Seacombe landing stage. She was later refloated and after extensive repair put back into service.

There was extensive damage but few casualties in June. On 1st November, two fatal casualties in a bad raid. Heavy rain hampered rescue operations.

The last bomb fell on Merseyside on 10th January, 1942. The All Clear sounded which signalled the end of the ordeal and the people of Wallasey left their shelters for the final time.

The heroes are the men and women who were living through the horror of the blitz. Wallasey learnt the real meaning of total war.

30/32 Tollemache Street, November 1940

Top: Travellers Rest, Marine Promenade, 7-8 May 1941
Bottom: St. Albans Road, 1940

Top: Corner of Rowson Street and Field Road
Bottom: Erskine Road, March 1941

Top: Mount Pleasant Road viewed from Pleasant Street, 31.08.40
Bottom: Mount Pleasant Road nos 155-157, 31.08.40

Top: Earlston Road
Bottom: Manor Road

WHEN THE LAW PROHIBITED BATHING

Looking at 1909. No mixed bathing, and no bathing without a machine, The *Daisy, Crocus* and *Lily* among the flowers of the local Wallasey ferries. Hackney carriage stands, and a 621-foot tower at New Brighton. A village pump in Poulton and a Marine Parade in Seacombe. Horse-drawn fire engines and noisy smithies. All of them a part of the Wallasey of over a century ago.

Before it received its charter in 1909, Wallase's Chairman of its District Council. was Mr. William Henry Robinson.

The District Council, formed in 1896, had 30 members. The clerk was Mr. H.W. Cook. Its offices were at the corner of Church Street and King Street, Egremont. The telephone number was, appropriately, Wallasey 1.

In this year Princess Louise and the Duke of Argyle visited the Navy League Homes, in Withens Lane (the site of the former

Technical College).

It was the year the Isle of Man steamer *Ellen Vannin* was lost just outside the Mersey with all hands (35).

In the newspapers of the time people were reading about Bleriot's crossing the Channel by aeroplane, about the coming into force of old age pensions of 5s a week to men and women over 70.

Captain Howard E. Martin was the ferries manager. The tramways department was headed by Major R.R. Greene.

The ferries had 11 steamers, the Daisy, Crocus, Thistle and Lily among them and a large barrage (Emily) and a dredger (Tulip).

A year's ferry contract was 25s. A monthly contract was 2s 3d.

Luggage boats sailed every 40 minutes from Seacombe to Liverpool. Sailing times were "changed according to season and to meet the convenience and requirements of market gardeners and greengrocers."

The town had a population of 73,000. The death rate was the lowest for years : 12.7 per 1,000. There were 15 elementary schools (including St. Paul's, St. Mary's and Seacombe Wesleylan). The Education Department ran a house-wifery centre at 100 Littledale Road, Seacombe.

Formed just over 10 years before, in 1898, the public library in Earlston Road had branches at Demesne Street, in a shop at 374 Poulton Road, and at the corner of Leasowe Road and Wallasey Village. They were issuing about 225,000 books a year.

Bathing machines stood down on the sands, and there were regulations laid down for their use. You couldn't bathe just anywhere more than a century ago.

Females could use the machines near Holland Road and Rowson Street stretches of the sea front. Males went to the Magazine Lane or Waterloo Road areas.

The rules included the following: "A person of the male sex, above the age of 12 years, shall not approach within 20 yards of any place at which any person of the female sex may be set down for the purposes of bathing, or at which any such person may bathe."

Wintry scene of Seaview Road at the turn of the 20th Century

It was forbidden to bathe without "tent, screen, shelter or bathing machine" between the hours of 8 a.m. and 8 p.m.

Boats could be hired for sailing on the clean, unpolluted waters of the Mersey. They coast 1s 6d per hour for three persons.

Horses and ponies could be hired on the sands for a shilling an hour. A donkey cost half of that.

There were hackney carriage stands at Seacombe Ferry, Egremont Ferry and New Brighton.

At New Brighton they had just knocked down the Ham and Egg Parade that had got the place a bad name up to 1907. Victoria Gardens was being put in its place.

As mentioned in an earlier chapter, New Brighton still had its tower, 621 feet.

The Winter Gardens Theatre, just opened, was staging operas, plays and variety.

Poulton still had its village water pump and trough in 1909.

They stood right in the centre of the cross-roads of Poulton Road, Mill Lane, Breck Road and Poulton Bridge Road.

Seaview Road, Liscard, was still a rough country lane, guarded on one side by a high brick wall.

Trafford House stood on the site of the old General Post Office in Liscard Village, and Mill Lane had a mill pond with a farmhouse on its banks.

Egremont had its long pier, its 'Hen and Chickens' pub, and Garner's Farm, in Rice Lane.

Seacombe had tightly-packed property known as the Mersey Street area, and a gateway in Birkenhead Road with the word 'Marine Parade' over it, carved on a painted board.

Oakdale Road was a dale and north from the top of Borough Road fields stretched away towards Liscard.

There were smithies in all parts of the town, noisy with the ring of anvils.

Horses drew the local fire engines. The stables were on the corner of Seaview Road and Liscard Village and was the former site of the Capitol Cinema, Liscard.

There were weekend concerts in the old band stand in Central Park. There were one-man bands in the streets.

Poulton was famous for its long lanes of trees. Seacombe and Wallasey Village had small cottages with huge flower-filled gardens.

There were fields and stretches of water that have long since been built over. The trees have gone, and the cottages with the big gardens have gone too. The old stiles, wooden gates and manor houses of Liscard and Poulton have crumbled to dust.

World War One was to mark the beginning of big changes in the town. Wallasey was to branch out, stretch itself, give itself a new look.

OLD COTTAGES, MANORS AND QUIET CORNERS

Little courts and alleys, crowded and gas-lit. Stiff Victorian terraces. Cottages hidden round leafy corners. Big houses importantly guarded by ivy-covered walls and thick hedges, and with their tradesmen entrances plainly marked. Almost all of them gone now, swept away on the great tide of growth and change and progress. Gone with the old cobbles, the horses and carts, the rattling trams and the quaint old names.
Diesel buses purr along the broad roads where fields used to be. Asphalt and concrete where once were winding lanes, cart tracks and farm gates.

Seaview Road looking up towards Mount Pleasant Road, c1900

Although it had assumed the dignity of a county borough in 1913, the Wallasey of just over a century ago was still a scattered community, a collection of villages.

The place was in its municipal infancy. It was full of farmsteads, fields, quiet spots, and charm.

Lace-curtained little dwelling-places that were pretty and highly individual. Mansions that were solid and four-square.

It was just before the outbreak of World War One which was to see the start of clearance orders and road-widening schemes that would completely alter the face of Seacombe, Liscard, Wallasey Village and Poulton.

Pavements in the old days were narrow. There was a partiality for lots of steps to the houses that stood off them, houses with fussy ornaments in their fanlights and plants in their front windows.

Occupiers of little houses competed with one another to make their front steps the brightest. Yellow stone and elbow grease were in evidence every morning,

Nelson Gutter, later renamed as School Lane, Wallasey Village, c1890's

---

The smallest and meanest places had their bright brass knockers and carefully laundered curtains.

In Seacombe there was the Mersey Street area. Not far away, close to Demesne Street, was a court known locally as Little Hell.

Along the Dock Road were cottages with flower filled gardens, poultry runs and carved wooden gates.

Wheatland Cottage was in Kelvin Road, which was then a cul-de-sac. The cottage overlooked fields towards the flour mills in Dock Road.

At the junction of Gorsedale Road (once known as Cinder Lane) and Gorsey Lane stood Old Manor Farm. Fields sloped down to Wallasey Pool.

A brisk walk away at Poulton was The Eyrie, the big house up on the Breck.

Its neighbour was Darley Dene, demolished in the air raids of 1941.

Up in Liscard was Urmson's House. It gave its name to Urmson Road. Built in 1729, it was demolished in 1928.

Not far away was Clifton Hall. It stood next to Wallasey Grammar School, in Withens Lane, became a sea training home, and later was taken over by the Corporation to form the start of the Technical College.

NEW BRIGHTON LIFEBOAT

One Hundred Years of History

1860s – 1960s

New Brighton Lifeboat Station is more than 150 years old. The history of the station is a long one, and rich in many stories of heroism and achievement. There has been a lifeboat at The Magazines, in Wallasey, for many years before the decision in 1863 to station a new lifeboat at New Brighton. The boat, the 'Rescue', was launched on 24th January. It was tubular shaped and decidedly modern for its time.

The boat was 42 feet long, eleven and a half feet wide, and rowed fourteen oars. Back in 1863 a crowd of 70,000 people watched it launched in Liverpool.

In 1868 the New Brighton station was completely reorganised and the boat was substantially rebuilt and renamed as the 'Willie and Arhur'. In the April of that year a new 'self-righting' lifeboat was added called the 'Lily'. Together with a new large wooden boathouse, both boats would make many dramatic turn-outs and errands of mercy.

In July, 1894, the Mersey Docks and Harbour Board, until then responsible for life-saving services in the Mersey and its approaches, transferred all local lifeboats to the Royal National Lifeboat Institution.

Norman B Corlett, RNLI, 1967

By the 1960's there had been fifteen boats in use at New Brighton. All but two of these were outright gifts or purchased with legacies left for the purpose.

Famous among them was the 'Queen', operated between 1897 and 1924, 'William and Kate Johnson', 1924-1950, and 'Edmund and Mary Robinson,' 1938-1950.

These three boats alone between them saved 524 lives. They attended scores of vessels in distress.

Two boats were continuously on call at New Brighton from 1863 to 1950 when the establishment was reduced to one.

'Norman B. Corlett,' cost £31.000. It was presented to the station by Mr. W.E. Corlett and family in memory of his son who lost his life in local waters. H.R.H. The Duchess of Kent named the boat at Liverpool in March 1951.

The 'Norman B. Corlett' was the biggest and fastest of all the lifeboats that had served since its establishment at New Brighton. She was withdrawn from service in 1973.

Originally the station was based at the New Brighton Landing Stage but by 1974 the new boat house was built at the bottom of Atherton Street, which had previously been the Marine Park Day Nursery.

MARKET GARDENING IN WALLASEY

Between 1850-1914 part of the low lying land west of Wallasey Village became famous for its market-garden produce. The beginning of this can however, be traced back to the end of the eighteenth century for a certain Thomas Hedge, reporting in 1794 on agriculture in Cheshire refers to the success of market gardens at Wallasey even at that date, saying "the improved method, or what is yet called the secret, of raising early potatoes was first practised in this country by one Richard Evans, late of Wallasey in Wirral". Later, after describing the method of cultivation, he states "Early potatoes have been as plentiful in Liverpool market for some years past in the middle of May as they used to be in the middle of June".

During the latter part of the nineteenth century, the demands of the increasing population of Merseyside together with the provision of better facilities, resulted in the development of a zone of market-gardening by the pioneering efforts of members of the Deane family and many others. This zone occupied the most fertile area of land in the Borough namely, that part of Wallasey Village between Leasowe Road and Green Lane. Here, the land is low lying and protected from one encroachment of the sea by the sand-hill belt. It slopes very gently towards the Birket or Fender river and has an open, southern aspect. The soil, resulting from the mixture of the blown sand and the alluvial clay. was a light, sandy loam to which has been added repeated application of farmyard or stable manure until now it has the rich dark colour of fertile peat or "moss-land". The presence, in small quantity, of salt in the soil also favours the market-gardening activities.

Climatically, too, the region is favoured. The mild, equable conditions and the relative freedom from frost combine with a fairly even rainfall regime and a slightly salty atmosphere to produce a great variety of vegetables, including early potatoes, asparagus, tomatoes, lettuce etc. Added to these natural advantages of soil and climate, is the protection afforded from the strong sea winds by the thorn or privet hedges that divide the land into small patches. These hedges had been considerably strengthened by the accumulation of hedge clippings and vegetable refuse reinforced where necessary by straw-plaiting to form an almost impenetrable bulwark.

In these market-gardens it was usual to obtain four or five and, on occasion, even six crops per year from the same patch of land. The produce was of high quality and readily finds a market in Liverpool, as it did likewise during the nineteenth century. A valuable market is also provided by the demands of liners and cargo boats sailing from Liverpool. Wallasey tomatoes and, to a lesser extent, potatoes also find numerous purchasers in the London market.

THE WALLASEY FROG MAN

Featured in the picture overleaf is Ian Fraser, the Wallasey V.C., and his frogmen, at the reopening of the New Brighton Bathing Pool on Saturday, 17th May 1947. Ian won the V.C. in 1945 for a gallant and successful midget submarine attack on a Japanese cruiser. A demonstration of an attack on a ship was given in the pool, the operation being followed with keen interest by a large crowd. Left to right: The Mayor (Alderman B.C. King), Ian Fraser, V.C., Brian Fraser (his brother), Bob Francis, and the Baths Manager, Mr. C. Mitchell. Ian passed away on 1st September 2008. Part of the New Brighton promenade is named in his honour.

It is also worth mentioning that two Wallasey men took part in the British Commando raid on St. Nazaire in March 1942. The Wallasey men were former Commando Sergeant Fred Holt, of Wallasey Road and Mr. Leslie Whelan, of Leander Road. Both were amongst the 127 survivors of the raid who were taken prisoner and spent the rest of war in German prison camps. Fred passed away in 1964, aged 49. Leslie died in 1979, aged 63.

WALLASEY AND THE GREAT WAR

1910 saw Wallasey get its Charter – it was the first borough created by George V. The King had been reigning for just over two months when he signed the Charter of Incorporation on 19th July, 1910. It was a turning point in the story of the town. However, the important document was despatched from London by ordinary mail. It arrived on 19th July. There was no band to meet it. No large scale celebration for such an important scroll. Since the turn of the 20th Century the somewhat scattered community had been welding itself together. Liscard, Poulton and Seacombe had ceased to be separate and rather insular villages. They began to link together.

New Brighton, glorying in a 621 foot tower higher than Blackpool's had lived down the notoriety of its old 'Ham and Egg Parade'. A place for day trippers was becoming a real resort,

By 1910 the Edwardian era had come to an abrupt close with the death of Edward VII. Big, new, exciting things were happening in the world, and Wallasey was touched by the effect of them.

The first few years of the decade was to see many changes. Growth was the thing. Changes were happening. It became years of pursuit and endeavour.

The four years before the outbreak of the First World War was a time of expansion. The fields and the farms as well as the old cottages were disappearing as the builders were busy locally. Foundation stone laying and development made a quiet and almost semi-rural backwater to become a town taking itself seriously.

Wallasey became a County Borough in 1913. It started to become self-confident and fiercely independent municipality, determined to get ahead, proud of its new-found civic dignity. As a town, Wallasey had arrived.

King George V and Queen Mary were Wallasey's first Royal visitors when they visited the town on 25th March, 1914. A military escort trotted alongside as they drove in an open carriage to Central Park from the old Penny Bridge, where they were watched by a crowd of over 40,000 people as the King pressed an electric lever which set in motion machinery which lowered the foundation stone of the new Town Hall, being built in Brighton Street.

The Town Hall cost £150,000 to build and furnish. Originally other sites had been considered including Rake Lane, Marine Promenade and Liscard Village but Brighton Street site was voted as the site chosen. It was built by Messrs. Moss and Sons Limited in brick and covered with Derbyshire stone from Darley Dale Quarries.

The new Council was keen for new development and all seemed set for great growth and opportunities when the Great War broke out in August which brought everything to a halt.

By 1916 the new Town Hall was converted into a hospital for wounded soldiers. Over 300 beds were placed in rooms and corridors. Over 3,500 wounded soldiers passed through the makeshift wards.

There was much German resentment in Wallasey. Shops in Seacombe were vandalised. Bricks were thrown through shop windows which had served the community for many years before the war.

Wallasey during the war saw sentries on duty with fixed bayonets at Fort Perch Rock. Civilians had to keep well away. Soon after war was declared a Norwegian sailing ship had ignored messages from the fort. The commander issued orders to fire a warning shot but the gun had too much elevation and the shell sailed over the ship and landed at Hightown sandhills. Another shell was fired and this time it hit a vessel lying at anchor.

In 1918 two ferryboats, the 'Iris' and 'Daffodil', took part in a daring raid on Zeebrugge and returned covered in glory.

The local newspapers would list the many casualties of young men who would never return from Mons, Gallipoli and the Somme. The brutality of the war would see 848 men die from France, Middle East and beyond. These were dark, sad and shadowed years. The decade began so well with high hopes but Wallasey lost much in township and heroic men and women.

THE NEW BRIGHTON OPEN AIR BATHING POOL

The open air bathing pool opened on 13th June, 1934 by Lord Leverhulme and was described as the largest bathing pool in the world. In its first summer of opening almost one million went through the turnstiles. In its 56 year history little changed. The storm of 1990 saw its demise and its eventual demolition.
The following images are from the opening of the swimming complex:

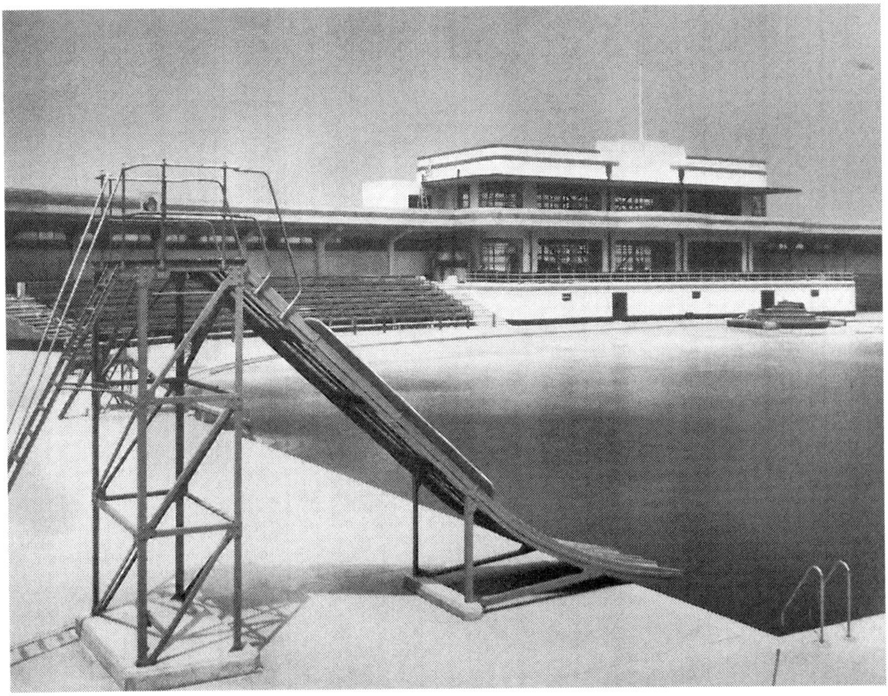

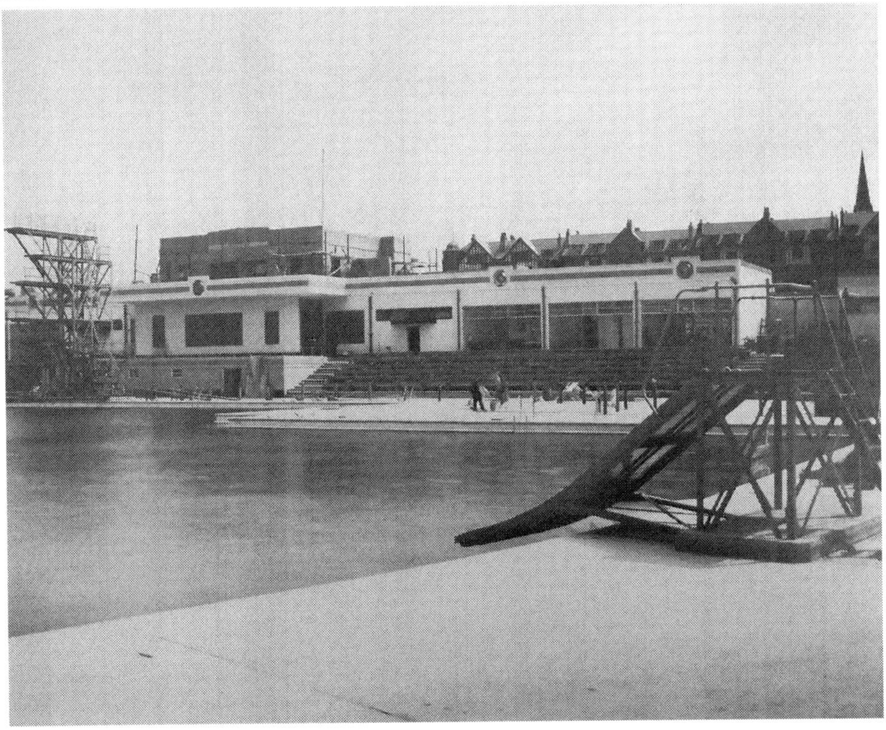

Above : Open Air Baths toilets with one penny turnstiles , 1934

Below: The Open Air Baths men's toilets, 1934

A VIEW FROM THE TOWER

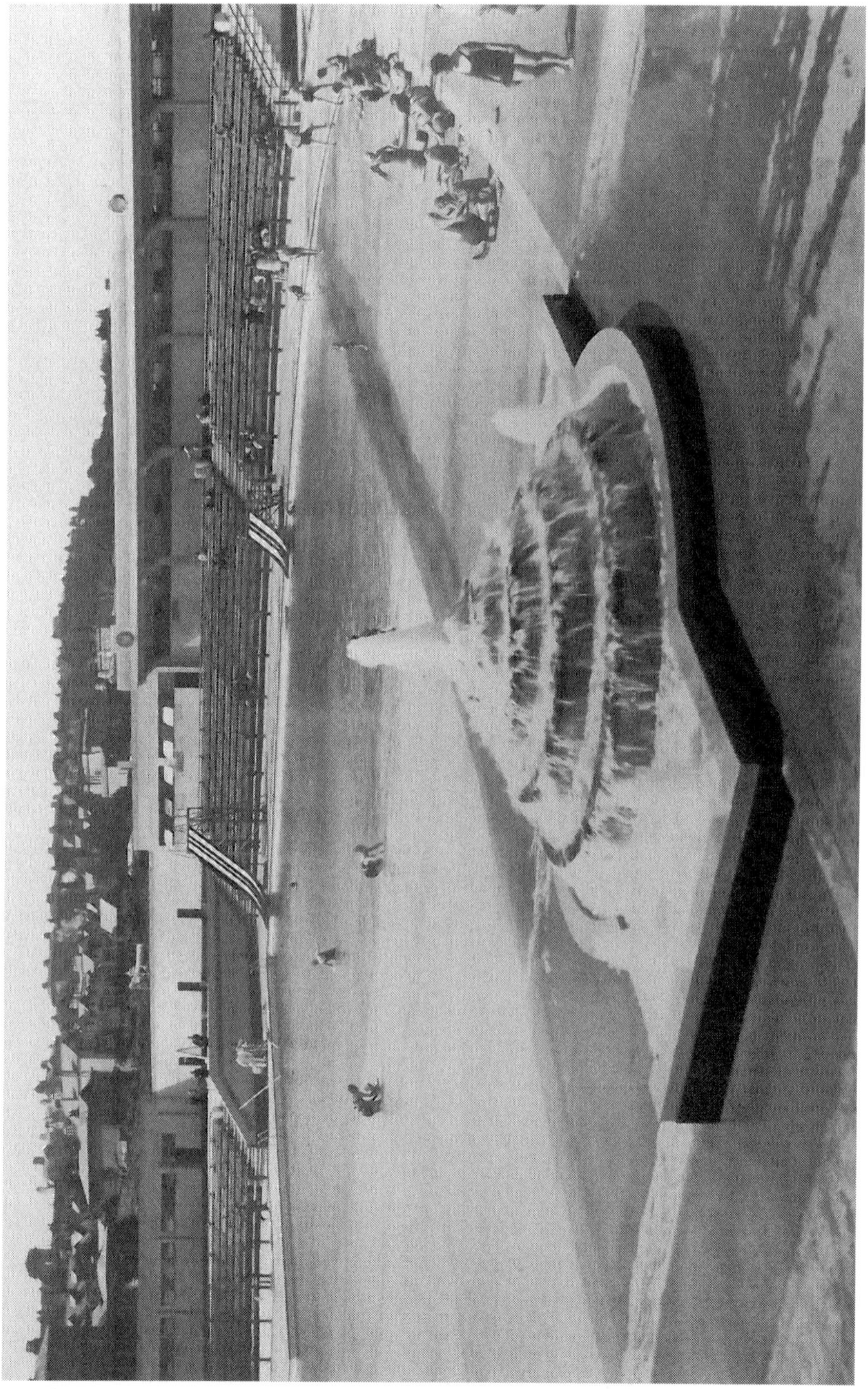

THE DARK TOWN BRIGADE

The Dark Town Brigade was the name they gave Wallasey's first fire-fighting service. Part-time, volunteer, and poor in equipment. A brigade that began with a handcart and a ladder, and that had to go to a cottage to collect the key to a 'station' that was little more than a shed. A brigade that was to become brave enough to take on the worst in fire and terror that bombs could shower down in war. The pioneer 'Dark Town' men started a great tradition.
The brigade was voluntary up to about 1900. The men drew a small retaining fee. The town's first fire station stood on a site fronting Mill Lane Water Tower. It housed one handcart and a leather reel the only one in Wallasey. There was a scaling ladder or two, some stand pipes, and a 40-foot wheeled escape. Smith's

Cottage, in the vicinity of the corner of Dinmore Road, was where the station key was kept. Captain Leader, outdoor head of the local water department, was the chief officer.

Wallasey firemen ready for a May Day parade in the early twentieth century. The horses are decorated with flowers. A top-hatted gentleman stands on the engine.

The firemen practised every Saturday afternoon. The bell rang. They all rushed out. The local children regarded the whole thing as enormous fun. And so, it was said, did certain of the firemen.

A wagon was acquired in the 1890s, and Messrs. Gibbons, of Liscard, provided the horses to draw it. The stables were on the old site of the Capitol Cinema, corner of Seaview Road and Liscard Village. Branches of the brigade were formed in Seacombe, under a tobacconist named John Howarth, of Brighton Street, and in Wallasey Village, under a water inspector, named Abraham Halewood.

Arrangements for calling the men and their equipment out where somewhat vague. The 'Dark Town Brigade' deserved its nickname. In due course a building was erected on a site at the bottom of Manor Road at the Liscard Village end. There was stabling and a yard.

Equipment grew, and included a manual fire engine, long ladders, and more up-to-date hoses. The engine was last used at a fire at new Brighton Tower in 1898. In that particular blaze a Fireman Shone lost his life.

The Tower, 621 feet high, had just been completed and opened to the public. The young fireman, a volunteer from Seacombe, fell 90 feet while fighting a blaze among the girders. Shortly after the tragedy moves were made to put the brigade on a more efficient footing. A growing town realised that it needed a better fire service.

For the first time a full time paid superintendent and a full-time engineer were appointed to control the nine auxiliaries who were available to be called out.

The station in Liscard was extended to include a duty room and a new house for the steam engine. A summons bell was put on the top of the station. In later years it was used to signal closing time for Central Park. There was a horse-drawn chemical engine, with a 60-gallon cylinder. The brigade took on its strength an ambulance, which up to that time had been operated from Gibbon's in Liscard.

A fire sub-station was established in Platt Street, Seacombe, where Messrs. Kenna's supplied the horses.

1912 saw the arrival of two motor engines, one fitted with a 60-foot extension ladder, the other with a wheeled escape.

More men were appointed on a permanent basis, and loan sanction was obtained for the Central Station that once stood in Liscard.

In 1914 the brigade was taken over by the police administration. On October 23rd of that year the Liscard station, with its 58-foot tower, was formally opened.

The establishment of a proper fire service came at a time Wallasey was becoming a bustling township, when the scattered 'villages' of Seacombe, Poulton and New Brighton were being wielded into a borough of importance. The service was really put to the test in the 1920s. There were several big fires in the town.

The worst was the vast blaze that gutted the Gandy Belt works in Seacombe in February, 1927. In 1931 came the fire that destroyed the old Lyceum Cinema in King Street. It had originally been a church. Later it became the Unit 6 and today the site is occupied by flats.

At the outbreak of war in 1939, 400 members of the Auxiliary Fire Service were enrolled as full-time firemen and in August 1941, all fire services were nationalised to make the most efficient use of men and material to combat fires caused by enemy action.

Horse-drawn engines and push-it-up-ladders. A cameraman c1905 got the firemen to pose outside the Mariners' Home, Egremont.

In the long, dark months of the air raids that came in 1940 and 1941 the Wallasey brigade wrote the proudest chapter in its long story.

Aided by the waters of the Mersey and the Dee glistening in

the moonlight, German bombers visited Merseyside time and again, dropping incendiaries to light a beacon target for the high explosives carried by heavier aircraft following on. The first bombs fell on Wallasey on August 19th, 1940. The long ordeal had started. Between August, 1940, and January, 1942, there were over 500 alerts.

In addition to 340 townspeople killed, 275 were seriously injured. The town was brutally battered night after night. In the raids, over 650 high explosives were dropped on it, over 1,000 houses destroyed, and over 17,000 houses damaged. Fires raged everywhere. There were weeks when the fire-fighters went almost completely sleepless. With the other Civil Defence workers, and with the families in the dimly-lit shelters, they took an excursion into hell.

In the blackest period of the blitz, in March, 1941, the water supply failed. It was the grimmest moment of Wallasey's war. But the fire and A.R.P. services kept themselves alive. They went on working. They won through.

The fire brigade came under local control again in April, 1948. It harnessed all the new fire-fighting aids, completely modernising.

PROGRESS THAT SWEPT AWAY OLD WALLASEY

The quiet corners of years ago have long gone. The fields and lanes that broad highways and vast estates have been wiped out. The farms and the white cottages that the march of progress overtook and trampled down. The places known by nicknames – Nelson's Gutter, Creekside, Suicide Lane, Cuffy Lane, Cinder Lane, and Golacre Meadow. Places that are now nothing more than names or pictures found in photo albums.
Successive road widening schemes in the 1920's and the 1930's, and the blitzes of the early 1940's, changed the face of the town. Much was swept away that had character, colour and charm.
The cottages of Liscard and Seacombe, Poulton and tree-rich

Wallasey Village, were pretty and small, highly individual. Lace curtains, and flowers all around.

Mona Cottage stood until 1924 at the corner of Rake Lane and Liscard Village. It was sometimes called Oyster Shell Cottage, for its window mullions were covered with the shells.

There was Finnegan's Cottage, close to Rice Lane, Egremont. It stood until 1925, a one-storey place of whitewashed walls.

There were windows at each end, but none at the sides. The roof timbers were mostly masts or spars of vessels.

Down in Seacombe were Concertina Cottages, equally as picturesque. They had been built in 1875.

The form of construction was most unusual. The houses were hexagonal in shape, built in five blocks of three.

They covered an area just to the south of St. Joseph's Church, in Wheatland Lane, and were demolished in 1954.

Between Victoria Road (now Borough Road) and Brougham Road, near the top and approached by a noble of avenue stood Winch House. It disappeared some 130 years ago.

Zig Zag Hall stood on the site now occupied by Steel Avenue and Sheen Road. Large and barn-like, it could be seen up to 100 years ago.

Up to the early 1920s Mill Lane really had a mill pond. On its bank stood a farm. Locals use to go fishing in it, sailing on it in a little boat, and picnicking on its grassy banks. The site is now occupied by the corner of Eldon Road.

A quarter for the wealthy was old West Seacombe Terrace, now Percy Road. The houses were large. Each had its servants' quarters. From it there was a clear view of Bidston Hill. Green fields stretched towards the docks. There use to be a pleasant rustic walk down Oakdale to the Dock Road, leading on to a path across the marsh to Bidston.

Westland House, Percy Road, c1912

Gorsedale Road was known as Cinder Lane. At its intersection with Gorsey Lane stood Old Manor Farm. Little bridges crossed several creeks.

Running up from the Dock Road near Gorsey Lane was Creek Side, a name recalling that Wallasey Pool was not always confined between dock walls. Near it was Robinson's Creek.

A footpath, nicknamed Suicide Lane, ran across the fields to Seaview Road, along the route known today as Kingsway. Love Lane, a charming tree-shadowed walk, was called Cuffy Lane, because it bordered a field called Cuff Hey. Golacre Meadow stood nearby.

School Lane, in Wallasey Village, answered to The Gutter. Rice Lane housed the well-known Garner's Farm.

Until Seabank Road was cut through the fields, King Street (at one time Barn Lane) ended at Green Lane (now Greenwood Lane). Few of the fine old houses are left. Years ago the town was quite famous for its miniature mansions.

Concertina Cottages, 1954

One of the first to be built was Poulton Hall. Handsome and four-square in style, it went up in 1790 and came down in 1933. Poulton Hall Road stands where it did.

On the site of the Town Hall was North Meade. Its grounds extended from Brighton Street to the river wall.

Another fine house was Liscard Castle. The title was misleading. It never was a castle, although its battlements and stone lion embellishments gave it dignity.

It stood near the end of Seaview Road. Built in 1841, it was demolished in 1902. The locals called it Marden's Folly.

The house was originally occupied by a Mr. John Marsden, a brush manufacturer in Liverpool. A big, eccentric-looking place.

It was finally divided into three parts, the Turrets, the Towers and the Castle. Roads bearing two of these names now mark the site.

The fine old "Stonehouse," on the site of the present Stonehouse Road, crumbled to a heap of bricks and dust about 100 years ago. Its history went back to the 1600s.

Change in the town was sweeping in the 1920s and 1930s. Plans and clearance orders altered the place dramatically.

Now there is hardly a street or road which stands exactly as it did. The cottages, the winding lanes and the manors have gone. The ponds have been filled in. the pasture land has vanished.

Heavy traffic run along broad roads where quiet corners were. Asphalt, bustle and noise where trees and cart tracks used to be. The quaint, the picturesque, the quietly pleasing belong to the past.

As much a part of another world, another way of life, as gas-lamps, antimacassars, what-nots in the hall, and fussy bobbies on plush carpets.

Cottages that crumbled. Manors that melted into the stuff of memories.

A WALLASEY LANDMARK.

STROUDE'S CORNER.

THE TEST OF TIME.—*We have been here during five reigns. In the days of Victoria when our Borough was a place of green fields and scattered hamlets we served the people of Wallasey. To-day we are busier than ever.—Need more be said.*

B. J. STROUDE & CO.,

Drapers and Furnishers,

CORNER OF RAKE LANE & MAGAZINE LANE,

UPPER BRIGHTON, WALLASEY.

PHONE: WALLASEY 524.

WALLASEY IN THE 1920'S

The Twenties in Wallasey were busy and bustling. Years of enterprise and endeavour. In the decade of the Charleston and cloche hats, the town built and expanded and prospered. In the era of the 'flapper', the town really found its feet. It started going places.

Municipally, Wallasey got over the Great War pretty quickly. It was anxious for progress, ready for change.

Up went the first of the Council estate (the very first was at Alderley Road, in 1920/21). Up went more cinemas to greet the miracle of the 'talkies'.

New Brighton got itself a bigger pier. Motor buses (with solid tyres) began to replace the old tram-cars – but Wallasey missed the bus by failing to get itself included in the Mersey Tunnel scheme.

Gorsey Lane looking towards Poulton Road, 1925

In 1928, thirsty for expansion, the town embraced Moreton and took it under its administrative wing. It added an area which was eventually to become its main development interest.
They opened Oldershaw Schools – a bold experiment – and new libraries. The Rakers were born.
Sport and schools. Buildings and a widening of the borough boundaries.
The energetic Twenties. The full-of-go Twenties.
Much excitement greeted the introduction of the motor bus service (single-deckers, solid tyres). It began on April 1st, 1920, and the first route was from Seacombe Ferry to Harrison Drive.
An old Wallasey resident recalled in the 1960s of the tram-cars that ran in the early part of the 20th Century.
"You could go from Seacombe to New Brighton for a penny. At first there was no protection from the weather for the drivers. They drove the tram standing up, clad in oilskins, sou' westers and leggings. It was a tough job."
Tram-car rides through Liscard had a stopping place near the 'Monkey House'. It was a pagado-like public shelter which stood

where the traffic lights are today (opposite the Duke's pub). Underneath it were public conveniences.

The shelter was removed in 1926. The conveniences stayed until the 1930's.

You could get a ferry across the Mersey for 1s.6d. weekly contract. The boats of the time were the original 'Iris' and 'Daffodil', and the 'Liscard' and 'Farley'.

In the middle years of the decade they started building houses along and off Leasowe Road. Until that time it had been an area of fields and farms, with here and there white-washed cottages.

Moreton was notable for floods and asbestos bungalows. Mushroom growth of shacks and chalets got it a bad name. They called it 'Shanty Town'. A clean-up started when Wallasey took over.

Cinemas had a boom time of it in the Wallasey of a century ago. There was Valentino and Theda Baram Henry Edwards and Chrissie White, Clara Bow and Garbo.

'The pictures' found a voice in 1927. 'The Singing Fool' and 'Sonny Boy'. Al Jolson packing them in at the old Capital Cinema, the Tracadero, in New Brighton, and the 'Cosy Cosmo', in Wallasey Village.

There was Martin Harvey, Matheson Lang, Seymour Hicks and Lewis Casson at the Winter Gardens Theatre.

At the Hippodrome, in Seacombe (later the Embassy Cinema), there was repertory and Hetty King. For 'one night only', in 1924, Henry Ainley appeared at the Floral Pavilion. Gracie Fields, virtually unknown, was at the Tower Theatre a year later. Local shops were selling the loud speakers sets that towards the end of the 1920's replaced the cats-whisker receivers.

The General Strike was born at midnight on May 3rd, 1926. Between then and the 'call off' on May 12th, tram and bus services were suspended for a day and a half. Some stones were thrown, some windows were smashed, but, according to the local 'Wallasey News' at the time, there were few incidents here.

Busy Seacombe Ferry., 1926. No trams or buses because of the General Strike at the time

---

Fashion wise, Missus Wallasey was rather daring. The long dress was banished.

A poet commented: "Half-an-inch, half-an-inch shorter. Skirts are the same for mother and daughter, When the winds blow, both of them show, Half-an-inch, half-an-inch more than they oughter."

The 'Wallasey News' reported an air-ship spotted over the town in 1929. In the same year hundreds of local Boy Scouts trooped to see Baden-Powell at the great Arrowe Park Jamboree.

You could send your son to Wallasey Grammar School privately for £4 a term. You could buy a wind-up gramophone for £2.15s – and get six free records.

New-laid eggs for a shilling a dozen. A made-to-measure suit ("with a pair of plus-fours free with every order") cost £3.

"Comfortable lodgings. Full board" averaged 22s. a week. You could rent a house in Ennerdale Road, New Brighton, for £70 a year. You could buy a house in Grove Road for £720.

The national Press discovered us: "New Brighton, on the Cheshire coast, is going to become another Blackpool".

BATTLE OF THE BRICKWORKS

In the early 1870's a brickworks was established on the river front to exploit the valuable clay bank lying between Tobin Street and Maddock Road, a company being formed for the purpose.
Vast numbers of bricks were made and a large export trade arose. Flats would lie alongside the river wall and the bricks were wheeled to the side and dumped in. Many persons walking along the narrow river wall would stand and watch the work going on but there was always the danger of accidents.
In December 1877, the company at last decided to stop this encroachment, and they erected a barrier to prevent passing people from encroaching on the works. The Wallasey Local Board met and resolved to defend the rights of the public. The

Fire Brigade, under Captain Leather, was ordered to demolish the barrier. This was done on a Wednesday in December, 1877 the chairman of the Works Committee, Mr. Henry Skinner, announced in the Council that "the barrier, at the moment, was floating down in the neighbourhood of the lighthouse at New Brighton". But, even while he was speaking, another barrier was being erected. On Thursday the Fire Brigade again turned out and demolished it. But on Friday all night the brickmakers were at work and a very formidable barrier stood up against further attack. Huge beams had been thrown across the way, and spiked railings which could not be cut by axes or saws kept the attackers off the premises.

At 1 pm on Saturday a great crowd assembled at the foot of Tobin Street. The Fire Brigade, reinforced by a number of civilians, prominent among them being brickmakers who were opposed to the machine-made brickmaking, assembled in full force. Large axes were handed out to anyone willing to work and they marched to the brickworks entrance. Then the attack direct commenced. The tide was a high one and came well up to the wall. Two Liscard men, Jim and Bill Carney, well known "hard cases", commenced to attack the outer edge of the barrier, which overhung the river. All at once there was a shout and both of them were in the river. The defenders had a pole with a hook at the end. This they pushed through the spaces in the barrier and hooked the hackers into the river. They were soon fished out. Then big cross cut saws were brought into action to cut the baulks of timber. After some time, the defenders opened a hot water attack on the fire brigade. They had run pipes from the boiler along the top of the barrier about eight feet from the ground. These were pierced with holes, and when the water was turned on it was scalding hot and flew in all directions. A rush back took place, but the wily defenders had dug a trench about four feet deep, filled it with wet puddle clay, covered it with dust, and as the authority rushed out of the steam and water many sank up to the middle in the trench. Meanwhile, the attackers were getting on, until the defenders, who had prepared a lot of quarter bricks, began to hurl them. Thereupon the police, under Inspector Hindley, dashed in and arrested two of the directors, one of whom was Mr. Thomas Valentine Burrows, who afterwards lived to become alderman of the borough, Mayor, and had the honour of receiving King George V and Queen Mary when they came to open the Town Hall in 1914. Two of the workmen were also arrested for throwing stones. This was done to preserve order, and the matter was settled summarily on the Monday following by a fine. The result was that an arrangement was made between the Local Board and the Brick Company which preserved the right of way along the wall to the public.

Some years after the "Battle" there was an incident involving a young man named Henry Mayall, who lived in Church Street and was a member of the Egremont Institute. He was a well known long distance runner who went for a run late one evening along the shore and wall. At that time the wall was about three feet wide and much worn by constant traffic. There was no railing, so anyone who slipped might fall into the river or shore on one side, and on the inside the clay had been excavated six to eight feet and one could easily break a limb by falling there.

Next morning young Mayall was found dead on the shore. His legs had been broken from the fall and he drowned by the tide coming in over him. He was unable to crawl to safety and no one was about at that time of night.

As a number of accidents had happened before because of the unfenced wall there was great anger from the community so the Local Board was asked to take action to fence the wall. The clerk said that nothing could be done as the wall was the property of the Liverpool Dock Board and private.

But there were some persistent people behind the agitation, notably Samuel Boyd and Josiah Maximus Hawkins, a member of the Local Board for Seacombe. An interview took place with the chairman of the Dock Board, and ultimately permission was given to fence the wall and fill up and level the inside on condition that no damage was done to the structure of the wall.

This was done between Tobin Street and Maddock Road, and the public flocked down on Sundays and holidays. It was so appreciated that the Local Board extended it on to the Seacombe side between Tobin Street and Elmswood Road.

The Local Board decided that the whole of the local river frontage should be made available to the public.

Up to that time the whole of the frontage had been open to the shore. The acquisition and improvement of stretch after stretch of it was accompanied by the buying of as much as possible of the immediate background, in the interests of appearance and future control.

As well as being fantastic, noisy and colourful, that battle of the brickworks was a local milestone, From it came the 'push' the town needed to get on with the job of improving itself, of growing up.

Although they did not know it at the time, those angry stone-throwers at Egremont, nearly a century and a half ago, were the pioneers of the promenade, the sketchers-in of one of the most important chapters in the story of the rise of Wallasey.

GANDY
BELTING
For TRANSMISSION
and CONVEYING
TRADE
ESTD
1875
MARK
GANDY
BELTING
GANDY
BRAKE
LINING
"Safety
Grip"
Specify
GANDY
GANDY LIMITED · WALLASEY · CHESHIRE

A VIEW FROM THE TOWER

THE
GRAND HOTEL
MARINE PROMENADE
NEW BRIGHTON

BOLDLY situated on the sea-front and commanding magnificent views of the ever-changing panorama of river and sea . . . . an hotel of infinite charm, supreme comfort and personality.

DINE AND DANCE IN
The SPANISH RESTAURANT
DINNER DANCE NIGHTLY at 8 p.m.

Britain's Brightest Cocktail Bar

Open to Non-Diners

FULLY LICENSED.

For Reservations write or 'phone Wallasey **2243**.

Appointed by the Automobile Association.

THE HERMIT OF WALLASEY

Frederick Krueger was a man of mystery. A mystery story in old Wallasey. Everyone spoke about him, but few knew much about him. Frederick Krueger was seldom seen by the locals.

What do we know about the Hermit of Wallasey? Krueger lived in a ramshackle hut in Leasowe, near the sandhills from the mid-1870's. He spoke four languages. He was a graduate of as many German universities. He was a writer and composer. A tribe of dogs lived with him and he had hundreds of books as well as a grand piano for company. He was the local character.

Krueger lived at a time when Leasowe was fields and farmsteads. There was little cottages, ponds and small pubs. The air, redolent of farmyards and hay, together with the sights, sounds and scents of agriculture, and the comparative absence of wheeled traffic, imparted an atmosphere of rural life.

He was a reclusive man and died in squalor and yet when he died scores of Wallasey Villagers clubbed together so that he might not be buried in a pauper's grave.

Krueger first arrived in Wallasey in about 1878. After ten years spent living in make-shift dwellings on various sites, he took over a corrugated iron hut near Green Lane, then a hedge and tree bordered track. He was described as being "very hunched, a Bohemian type, with a drooping moustache."

In early 1905 Krueger gave an interview to a newspaper reporter. In the article he revealed that he received an allowance from Germany, just enough to maintain him.

"I have no friends." He said at the time, "I wish to exist alone. All I desire is the right to pass my days in study and contemplation. Only that."

The reporter found when visiting Krueger that the old man's hut had an extensive library. They were "books on classical subjects, in Latin and Greek." There was a great deal of music about "Mozart and Wagner and Krueger himself."

The hut Krueger resided in was about fifteen feet long, twelve feet high and six feet wide. It was a clutter, an eyesore." The reporter said "Mr Krueger lives, metaphorically speaking, in the clouds."

That interview was one of the very few contacts that Krueger made with the world outside. A few years later some of the mystery surrounding him was to be explained.

During the early weeks of March, 1909, no one had heard or seen Krueger for quite some time. The police had to force an entry into the hut where they found him dead. He had been dead for a week.

During the inquest many facts emerged about the dead man's background. Inquiries had been made at the German Consulate in Liverpool. Krueger was born in c1848 in Mecklenburg and christened Gothold Johann Friederick and had once been a soldier in Germany. He had graduated at Rostock, Munich and Leipzig Universities. For a time he had practiced law. His family had been on the personal staff of the Emperor of Prussia. Later information about him revealed that he had been something of a Greek and Latin scholar, and had mastered English, French and Italian. When he was younger he earned a considerable reputation as a concert pianist. Many of his own compositions were included in his programmes.

So why did Krueger abandon his culture that he had lived in and throw away a promising career when he was in his thirties? The secret died with him on a March morning over a century ago, in a ramshackle little hut near the Leasowe sands.

THE HOUSE IN THE PARK

Sir John Tobin, a Liverpool merchant and ship-owner, was born in 1762. He was Mayor of Liverpool in 1819 and was knighted by King George IV in 1820.

By the 1830's Sir John had retired and took up residence at Moor Heys House, later Liscard Hall and then the Collage of Art.

The fine manor house was surrounded by fields and gardens which later became Central Park. The estate had been laid out in the 1820's. The house once stood high and commanded a fine view of the surrounding countryside as well as views of the sailing ships on the River Mersey.

At the time of Sir John coming to Wallasey it was thinly populated and its inhabitants were engaged mainly in agricultural work. The population in the 1830's was 2,737, having increased by more than one hundred per cent since the 1821 census. The area was all green fields and lanes, with windswept sand dunes and marshlands to the north and west.

Sir John had his own fishing lodge, down where Sandon Road now joins the promenade at Egremont. It stood on the very edge of the river at a spot known then as Coding Gap. He had his own yacht in which he sometimes used to cross the river instead of using the paddle-driven ferryboats. Lady Tobin kept a telescope in a room at Liscard Hall, so that when it was stormy she could watch the yacht cross safely home from Liverpool.

Sir John had an eye for business. He forsaw that Wallasey Pool was likely to prove valuable and bought land on its banks, which he later sold to Liverpool Corporation. He was the builder and owner of the 1,150 ton *Great Liverpool*, a steamship launched in October 1838 and then considered a marvel in naval architecture. She was wrecked in 1846 off Cape Flintsterre with the loss of two lives.

In 1822 Captain Scoresby, commander of the Arctic whaler Baffin, honoured him by naming Cape John after him when surveying the coast of Greenland.

Sir John died on 27th February, 1851, at the age of 89. He was buried in the churchyard of St. John's, Egremont, the church he had built in 1833. He was so concerned about the spiritual needs of the people that were not provided for, he donated land on which St. John's stands and most of the money needed for the building.

Sir John's son, the Rev. John Tobin, was the first incumbent at St. John's. He lived at Liscard House which was built by his father at the junction of what are now Eaton Avenue and Ferndale Avenue.

Sir John's other legacy to the town was Egremont Ferry itself. He gave his backing to the founder of it, Captain John Askew, in his younger days the skipper of slave ships. Egremont was christened after Askew's birthplace, a small village in Cumberland. The parish of Egremont is covered in the next chapter.

Sir John was succeeded at Liscard Hall by his son-in-law, Harold Littledale, who was responsible for building Model Farm, in nearby Mill Lane. The history of the enterprise is covered in a later chapter – *'Wallasey's World Famous Farm'*.

On the death of Littledale on 9th March, 1889, Liscard Hall and its grounds were purchased by the Wallasey Local Board and thrown open to the public.

Since the 1860's the town had developed considerably. It had acquired shopping centres in Liscard and Seacombe. Busy builders had given it lots of small streets and terraces. Industry and boat building had gradually taken over from agriculture as the main fields of employment. The town was taking itself seriously. It was eager for expansion, anxious to go places.

Liscard Hall and its surrounding acres became the first major acquisition of the Local Board. Subsequent purchase of adjoining land gave the town a park of over 57 acres. The woods on the land gave way to lawns and tree-shaded paths. Tobin's gardens became flower beds and playgrounds. The old stables were used by the Parks and Gardens Department.

The fine old house became the Liscard Science & Art College. The college closed in 1982 and in 1988 became an employment training college. The end of the building came in July 2008 after a fire caused extensive damage. The structure was deemed unsafe and was demolished.

Harold Littledale

EGREMONT

Of all the parishes of Wallasey, Egremont is the youngest of the villages. It began down by shore in the 1820's when Captain John Askew, an investor in land and in his younger day's owner of slave ships, built a house for himself on land between what is now Sandon Road and Maddock Road.

He called the home "Egremont", after his birthplace in Cumberland. It was partly in Liscard and partly in Seacombe, and gradually the house gave name to the district.

In 1828 Askew built the first Egremont ferry. It was operated by little wooden paddle steamers. The ferry passed into various hands, and over 150 years ago was bought by the Wallasey Local Board. Improvements were made. Things began to look up.

The new floating stage was erected. There was a 'grid-iron' on which boats could be repaired.

In May, 1932 a large oil tanker, the *British Commander*, broke away from her anchorage and came to rest against the pier, which was wrecked. Repairs were carried out and the ferry re-opened the following year.

This incident foreshadowed the end. In May, 1941, the pier was rammed, this time by the coasting steamer *Newlands*. Damage was extensive and no attempt was made to rebuild.

The last of the pier was dismantled in 1946 and the stone slipway beneath was blown up. The operation removed a landmark which had existed for more than a hundred years.

Last boats ran to Egremont in August, 1939. When World War Two came, the ferry put up its shutters. It was never to open again.

Egremont of the 19th Century consisted mainly of allotment gardens, cottages and small terraces. There were open fields from Brougham Road to Church Road.

Until Seabank Road was cut through the fields, King Street (formerly Barn Lane, but renamed after Ellen King, who owned the land) ended at Green Lane (now Greenwood Lane) and the first houses in Seabank Road had only fields in front.

The snooker hall on King Street was at one time the drill shed of the 3rd Cheshire Rifles and was built in about 1864. Later it became the Royal Cinema.

King Street was at first purely residential with the exemption of a few shops in Tobin Street. Manor Lane was a private road guarded with large stone pillars.

Withens Lane was probably given its name because it led to a field called The Withens. There is now a cul-de-sac off it called Withensfield, on the site of the old Withensfield House, which for many years was a school.

Trafalgar Road was formerly Abbott's Lane, after Mr. Abbott. Seabank Avenue had its own well and chain pump. Stringhey Road perpetuates another field name. At the north-west corner where it was joined by Marsden Road was the village well and pump.

From the bottom of Trafalgar Road to the shore was for many years just a strip of grassland. Zig Zag Road got its name from its tortuous course.

Steel, Littledale, Tobin, Walmsley and Scott are among roads in the district named after well-known residents of years ago.

Looming large on Tobin Street was the Egremont Institute, now demolished, formerly the Egremont Hotel. It was built in the 19th Century and patronised by Liverpool merchants and their families during the summer bathing season.

Close to it was The Long Pull, a little public house which got its name from the steep incline on which it stood.

And there was the Hen and Chickens, later called the Great Britain Hotel, King Street. Built in the early 19th Century and demolished in 1957. It was in a room at this old hotel that public mass was first celebrated in Wallasey, when Father John Just, of Liverpool, founded the parish of St. Alban's.

Standing on the corner of King Street and Trafalgar Road was a Presbyterian church. Later it became the Lyceum cinema until destroyed by fire in December, 1931. The Gaumont opened two years later. In 1974 the cinema became the Until 4 and finally the Apollo 6 before closing in 2000.

Before the building of the Town Hall, the old Council offices were in Church Street, near its junction with King Street. It was later used as a technical school until a German bomb during the blitz caused extensive damage and the building was demolished.

In Rice Lane was Garner's Farm and a large field occupied the land from Rice Lane to Rudgrave Square. It was a great place for picnics and Sunday School treats. Everyone knew the pretty spot.

At the corner of Rice Lane and what is now Greenwood Lane was a house called Springfield, with a garden running down to the top of Trafalgar Road. For some years the house was used as the vicarage for St. John's Church, hence the street called Vicarage Grove on its site.

The 1920's and 1930's brought changes to old Egremont. One by one the cottages began to disappear. The fields were built on. But it was the blitzes of World War Two that transformed the area. It was one of the heaviest-hit parts of the town. Church

Street, which had housed so much fine old properties, and which carefully looked after its trees, was almost flattened in the March of 1941.

Egremont, the once pretty village, full of the scent of flowers and of seaweed on the shore, was an ugly sight when the war ended. Gone are the fields and cottages but Egremont begun to build itself up into a new life. The 107 feet high Charter House apartments and new maisonettes was erected in the 1960's. Egremont began to stretch itself upwards.

IN AND AROUND EGREMONT: PICTORIAL

View of the beach at Egremont, c1912. Cliff House spire, Mariners Park, can be seen above the tree line

View of Trafalgar Road, 1950

Tobin Street, 1953. Egremont Institute at the bottom of the road

King Street junction with Burnaby Street with Great Britain pub on the corner, 1954

Stringhey Road with The Lord Nelson on the corner

At the junction of Church Street and Liscard Road the tramcar shelter, 1968

View of Egremont Pier, 1910

View of King Street, 1950's

Falkland Road, Egremont, c1910

SNOW BALLING AT SEACOMBE

Something a little different! When the shipbuilding yard of Messrs. Bowdler and Chaffer at Seacombe was in operation, it frequently happened that, when the snow was on the ground during the winter months, work was stopped. The men, having nothing to do, used to assemble in Victoria Road (today Borough Road), near the junction with Demesne Street and Abbotsford Street, and wait for persons making for the boats. These they would pepper with snowballs, and, in some cases get the people down on the ground and put snow down their necks. This went on for several years. Yet the authorities put no stop to it. Eventually in the winter of 1872 or 1873, one morning, a burly, powerful man, was just approaching the above named junction, when he saw a young clerk on the ground, and a number of men filling his neck and trousers with snow. He rushed forward and told them to let the young fellow up, and not to be so cowardly. They immediately turned upon him. There was no police about, and the magistrates in their carriages had been snowballed as they passed along to the ferry. The burly man put his back to the wall and used his stick to advantage. He saw one man aiming at him, and as he threw, the stick hit him on the hand and broke two fingers. Another man got a blow on the head which knocked him down and others bolted up the entry between the old Abbotsford Hotel and Mr. Andrew Davidson's, undertaker, establishment.

The police took action and summoned a lot of the offenders, and the magistrates inflicted fines of 40/- and costs on all. This put a stop to what had become a public nuisance.

WINSTON IN WALLASEY

On a bright Spring morning in one of the darkest years of Second World War, a man in a reefer coat and nautical cap, arrived in Wallasey. It was Friday, 25th April, 1941, when Winston Churchill visited the town. It was a brief visit which was supposed to be hush-hush. Top secret, but the word had got around. The crowds appeared from nowhere.
Wallasey and Merseyside were fighting one of the decisive battles of history – to keep open and working the greatest wartime port in Britain.
They were the days of tin hats, the black-out, and sand=bagged buildings. Shop and house windows wore criss-cross patterns of gummed paper, a protection against bomb blast.
Rations were small. A few ounces of this, a half-pound of that. Queues were long. British restaurants provided cheap meals to

the public. There was one in St. Paul's Road, Seacombe, another in Wallasey Village.

The town was urged by posters to remember that careless talk cost lives, and to save everything from water to scrap.

Five weeks before Churchill came Wallasey had gone through its worst raids of the war. With Birkenhead, it bore the brunt of a brutal attack. March 12th-14th 1941, were nights of fire and explosion and tremendous damage. The German bombers came over in waves. The raids were intense. The whole town was showered with incendiaries and high explosives.

The Prime Minister had come to see what a front-line town was contributing to the nation by its industry and its courage. The year before he had made his great "We shall never surrender" speech.

He stepped from an open car, accompanied by his private detective. He was escorted by the then Chief Constable, John Ormerod. There were also two or three dark-suited civil servants, and a small posse of policemen. No ceremony, no fuss.

He went along the Dock Road, waved to workers, and then drove on to Poulton. Civil Defence services were inspected. He saw heavily-blitzed Erskine Road. Churchill turned to the crowds who cheered him, gave then the V-for-Victory sign, and called out "God bless you all!" The car bumped over the rubble-strewn streets, moved slowly out of the town.

WALLASEY SMITHIES

In the days when horse power meant horses, Wallasey was full of smithies. Places noisy with the ring of anvils. Blacksmiths with spark-pitted arms.

The first picture (image 1) shows the smithy which stood over a century ago in Liscard Village. It was on a site roughly where the Post Office Delivery is today.

A.J Ince was the name on the signboard there. Business was brisk when horses pulled almost all the vehicles in the town.

The second image (2) shows the smithy in Smithy Lane, Seacombe. The whole site was demolished in the 1960's.

The horses lingered on into the age of wide roads, buses, the car invasion and the building of large estates, but each year in the 1920's and 1930's reduced their number. The sound of hooves on the roads of Wallasey is assigned to history. And the old smithies went with them.

image 1 : Ince Blacksmiths, Liscard Village, c1912

image 2: Blacksmiths in Smithy Lane, Seacombe, c1910

THE SEXTON AND THE FIRE

St. Hilary's Church stands on one of the highest points in Wallasey. The church has an unbroken history from the 6th Century. There has always been a church there. No remains have ever been found of the earlier church, but it is known that some rebuilding took place in the 1100's. In 1530 the tower was built, and this still stands today.

The church has been burnt on three occasions. Twice it was a church without a tower, and once a tower without a church.

The church that stands today was erected soon after the fire in 1857 which had completely destroyed the church built in 1757. It was in the early hours of 1st February, 1857, that the fire broke out. Crowds stood in the chill of the winter morning and watched it.

Although it was said at the time that smugglers in a cave underneath the church had been surprised by excise men and set fire to the building, the real culprit was reputed to be the sexton, John Coventry. For three or four Sundays the congregation had been complaining about the cold during services. The rector, Rev. Frederick Haggitt, asked the sexton to do something about it.

St. Hilary's Church, c1850

On the last occasion the complaints became a little too pointed. The sexton more or less said he would make it warm enough for them next week.

Having charge of the heating apparatus, he decided the evening before the fire to 'go to town'. He stoked the furnace to the top. But the heat came too soon. The distributing flues ignited part of the flooring. It was not until 2am on Sunday morning that the fire was discovered. By that time flames were leaping to the sky. The great glow could be seen for miles. Townsfolk were awakened by the roar of falling masonry. When the fire brigade arrived from Birkenhead – Wallasey had not then got one of its own – and an adequate water supply was obtained, all was hopelessly lost. The roof fell in. The proud peal of six bells smashed to bits on the floor. Only the tower was saved. Coincidentally, the fire occurred exactly 100 years after the church was built.

The Rev. Haggit was the hero of the occasion. At the risk of his life he dashed into the blazing inferno and saved the priceless old church records and parish registers. The accounts went back to 1658, the register to 1574, and in them was much to illustrate the daily life of the parish over the centuries.

The present cruciform shaped church was built in 1859. As for John Coventry? The local records tell nothing of his fate. There is one thing for sure – no one ever again complained of feeling cold as they sang their hymns and listened to the sermon.

The burnt out shell of St. Hilary's Church. 1857

WALLASEY VILLAGE

Wallasey Village is the oldest inhabited part of the town and it resisted change even though its neighbours of Poulton, New Brighton and Liscard were busily growing up. Long after the rest of Wallasey acquired a new look, the "Village" stayed a village. Only since the Second War World has the march of progress overtaken it.

Back in the old days Wallasey Village was a straggling line of small farms and cottages. There were crofts and closes, as well as narrow strips of arable land that ran up the hillside to Top Lane (now Claremount Road)

Up on the Breck stood Wallasey Mill. It was a landmark until the 1880's. The mill looked out over a Wallasey Village that had a thatched-roofed Cheshire Cheese, a tithe barn (on the corner opposite Leasowe Road), shippons and granaries.

172 Wallasey Village - Laburnum Cottage

From Top Lane fields stretched to Liscard and New Brighton. Lilac trees were everywhere. There were hedges and stiles.

At 171 Wallasey Village was a small cottage which served as the local post office. Willow Cottage, built in 1737, stood towards Grove Road.

The Sebastopol stood on the corner of St. Hilary's Brow and Breck Road. It was selling beer until 1930. The tiny Ring O'Bells stood at the corner of School Lane. Eventually it was to become a dwelling house. It was demolished over eighty years ago. The old Black Horse stood until the 1930's when the present hotel was built. At its side was the village mortuary. The original Lighthouse Inn had the reputation of being the smallest hostelries on the Wirral. Lighthouse Cottages stood beside it.

Wallasey Village was rich in pretty little places until road widening schemes and demolition orders caught up with it eventually. Gone are the quaint cottages – Laburnum Cottage, Anchor Cottage, Elm Cottage, Pear Tree Farm, Symond's Cottage.

The Cosy Cosmo, the Phoenix, Bigyard, the old pools and ponds, the cottages and the quaint tiny shops, are lost in the past.

View of Folly Lane looking towards Wallasey Vilalge, c1912

IN AND AROUND WALLASEY VILLAGE IN THE 1950'S: PICTORIAL

View of the old Lighthouse Pub from Green Lane, 1952

Wallasey Village, opposite the Black Horse, 1952

A VIEW FROM THE TOWER

Wallasey Village at the junction of Green Lane, 1952

Wallasey Village, looking south from near Big Yard, 1950

Wallasey Village, looking south from near St. John's Road, 1952

Wallasey Village looking towards Leasowe Road, 1950

Road widening near Big Yard, looking towards Leasowe Road 1951

Building of the Church of the English Martyrs, seen from Wallasey Village, 1952

A VIEW FROM THE TOWER

Wallasey Village looking south from top of Leasowe Road
29.10.1952

CYMBALS AT THE COUNCIL

Wallasey, like other places, has had some eccentrics on its governing body who have caused trouble and scenes at its meetings, but I doubt whether any place has had the unique distinction that Wallasey once had of a member using a musical instrument in defying the chairman's authority. In the early 1870's Mr. James Cowan, residing in Grosvenor Street, Liscard, and in business in Dale Street, Liverpool, was elected to the Wallasey Local Board. He was in a good way of business as a hatter, for silk hats were always worn by merchants. James was convinced there was a lot of bribery and corruption in Board affairs. He was always raising questions that were out of order, and, of course, had to be stopped by the chairman.

On one occasion, in 1872, when the Board refused to listen to him, James exclaimed, "Well, if you won't listen to me speaking,

I will make you hear me." Then, going to a table, he unfastened a large parcel which the members had been eyeing suspiciously all evening, and proceeded to clash an enormous pair of cymbals which he had brought with him purposely. He was then removed from the building.

James fell on bad times through neglecting his business for Board work and put his house in his wife's name. The qualification for a seat on the Board was that a member had to be rated to the poor on an assessment of £30 per annum, or that he was worth £1,000. The next time the chairman refused to accept James nomination as he had no assessment qualification, and it was believed that he was not worth £1,000. James brought an action at Chester Assizes and Mr. Justice Lush decided in his favour, saying that it was absurd to think that a man not worth a penny could enter the House of Commons while a trumpery Local Board required a monetary qualification. He held that, as the Act did not state £1,000 in cash, a man might have a picture of heirloom which he valued at £1,000. James won his case with costs. Later he turned his attention to the magistrates. The qualification for a County J.P. was that he must be rated to the poor on an assessment, and James attended at the Session House, Liscard Road (later The Continental cinema) and objected to certain J.P.s sitting. He was successful. Later two of the J.P.s had the assessment of the Cottage Hospital, Seacombe, and the Dispensary in Liscard Road placed in their names. When James attended at the Court to object he was ordered to keep silence under threat of committal for contempt of Court. It was held that the qualification was good though probably not bonafide. However, the qualification was removed very shortly after. James next escapade was to get himself nominated for the Local Board. The chairman refused to accept his nomination and also ordered that he should not be allowed to attend the counting of the votes. On the day of the counting James had been hiding across Church Street watching the public offices and the moment the doorkeepers had gone for tea he slipped across and went upstairs into the counting room where McAllister, the keeper of the building, heard the shout "Here we go again". A struggle emerged between James and McAllister. Eventually James was evicted from the building.

James was never again elected to the Local Board and passed away in 1921, aged 88.

Such a colourful character!

JOGGERS, TRAMS AND BUSES

Wallasey was somewhat slow in getting itself a properly organised transport system. It lagged behind its neighbours, such as Liverpool and Birkenhead.

As the population grew it became a matter of urgency to connect the ferries by transport between the 'villages' of Liscard. Wallasey and Poulton.

Wallasey Tramways Company was the first service to provide public transport. The first service began on 30th June, 1879. It operated over some two-and-half-miles of track between Seacombe Ferry, Liscard Village and Upper (New) Brighton.

These early horse-drawn omnibuses were known as 'joggers'. Passengers sat opposite each other on wooden seats. There was an oil lamp at each end of the car. There was no protection from the weather for the driver. He stood in front. The cars rattled and lurched at about fifteen miles an hour. The horses were always beautifully kept and had stables in Field Road, Upper Brighton

There were a number of privately-owned horse omnibuses that operated a service, mainly in the Seabank Road and Poulton Road districts. No service was provided by the Wallasey Local Board, although they had obtained powers to run a service. It was not until 1901 that the Board's successors, the Urban District Council, compulsorily purchased the tramways. They paid £22,670 for the lot which included seven cars and 78 horses.

Horse tramway on King Street, Egremont, May Day Parade, 1900.

Electric trams were introduced in March, 1902, and would rattle on with blue sparks flying for over thirty years. The Rake Lane route was the first to be introduced. Seabank Road and Warren Drive routes followed soon after. All cars at New Brighton approached the pier via Victoria Road and left by Virginia Road, Wellington Road and Rowson Street. The terminal lay-out was most unusual and was known locally as 'The Horseshoe'. The 'Horseshoe' was replaced in 1906 by a double track divided into four short spurs, after which cars approached via Virginia

Road and left via Victoria Road.

The first manager of the tramways was Colonel R. Greene. It was said that it was because of his name that the electric cars got the colour. When the contract for the cars was accepted, the question was asked what colour they should be painted. It was decided to leave it to the manager, and the reply was: "Oh, see Greene". And 'sea green' they became.

Even though the trams were a great success, the old villages of Poulton and Wallasey were still not connected from direct communication with the ferries until extensions were made in 1910/1911.

Each tram had indicators of their destination. 'S' stood for Seabnak Road, 'RL' for Rake Lane, 'WD' for Warren Drive, and 'P' for Poulton. Stoppage of the New Brighton and Egremont ferries during bad weather was indicated by flying blue and red flags on the trolley ropes of the cars.

By the end of World War One there was a gradual change from trams to buses. The first motor bus service, single-deckers on solid tyres, began on 3rd April, 1920. The first route was Seacombe Ferry to Harrison Drive, via Brighton Street, King Street, Seabank Road, Manor Rad, Liscard Village, Wallasey Road, St. Hilary's Brow and Wallasey Village. A 15-minute service was run from the start. The original buses were AECs with a seating for 32 passengers. They had wooden seats and were very uncomfortable on roads surfaces that were not very good. By 1924 improvements were made to the roads as well as the buses themselves. The first pneumatic tyred vehicles were introduced. Double-deckers came in. By 1930 they were carrying over twenty-four million passengers a year.

The success of the buses meant the end of the trams. The last of the electric trams ran from Seacombe Ferry to the depot in Seaview Road at mid-night on Thursday 30th November, 1933. It took a route along Poulton Road, Wallasey Village and Grove Road.

Their passing was almost an occasion of local mourning. They rumbled through a Wallasey that changed with every passing year. Through the country lanes in the early 1900's, through built-up areas in the bustling Twenties. The bone-shakers that helped to build the town.

Two trams pass each other in Liscard Village, July 1933.
The last journey of the trams.

AEC No.6. (HFF599). First introduced into operation in November, 1920.

SHANTY TOWN

At the beginning of the 20th century Moreton was looked upon as a poor relation to the rest of Wallasey. The area got the insulting nicknames of 'Shanty Town' and 'Shacksville'. The people who lived in the low-lying areas of Moreton often experienced flooding, especially in places like Kerr's Field, Meadowbrook Field and Fellowship Field. They lived in bungalows, old railway carriages as well as old buses. Though the houses were makeshift, the locals lived quite happily and there was a good community spirit. Water was provided by a stand-pipe and there was no electricity supply. There were no buses that ran to Wallasey and the nearest doctor was in Hoylake.

Deep mud and scattered cottages of *Bermuda Road, 1927*

Flooded water would often lap up against the dwellings which marooned families in their homes. The locals had to take a rowing boat through flooded water to go the shops. Even the postmen had to punt their way to deliver the mail.

Rainfall caused vast areas of mudded areas. Housewives took a towel in their baskets whilst out shopping. After wading through pools of water with shoes and stockings tied round their necks, they dry their feet and put their shoes back on again.

There was much resistance when Wallasey Council condemned the dwellings after becoming responsible for the area in 1928. By the outbreak of Second World War the properties were removed and the whole area cleaned up.

WALLASEY CRICKET CLUB

A few notes on the early years of the two most important clubs in the borough – Wallasey and New Brighton.

Wallasey C.C. is the elder of the two and should therefore come first, and it also bears the name of the ancient Village.

The club has had three lives. It originated first in a club which played down Leasowe Road, near the shepherd's hut which stood on the pathway leading across the links, an ancient highway at the junction with Green Lane – another old road. The land was let to the club by Mr. Harold Littledale, who generally had about 200 sheep and a number of young heifers on it. He had a pitch made for the club. The two gentlemen who created the club were Mr. Horspool and Mr. William McElroy. Two of the original members who joined on formation in 1867 were Mr.

Will George and Mr. Thomas Westcott. Mr. Horspool was the first captain and Mr. John Hortley first honourary secretary. The latter was the schoolmaster at Grammar School on the Breck, and about 1872 became Assistant Overseer and Poor Rate Collector for the Township of Liscard.

Later on Mr. James Harrison, of 'The Laund', laid out a pitch for the club on "Flynn's Piece", Grove Road, and Mr. Westcott became captain. This piece of land was public property on which the inhabitants were allowed to dig clay, and Major Walter, who lived at 'The Grange', objected to the public ground being used by a club, so he paid men to dig holes all over the pitch to prevent play.

The third venture was on the land on which the club now plays - The Oval, Rosclare Drive. Mr. John Braithwaite, a Yorkshireman, who lived at the top of Gerard Road became the captain. The land had been farmed by John Leicester, butcher, of Liscard, and he treated the club very generously, laid out a pitch, and charged little rent, which little was not always paid.

In 1870 there was a Cricket Club in New Brighton which played on a piece of land in Albion Street, now built upon, and lying abreast of St. James Church. Several members of the Wilson family, who lived in Rowson Street at the corner of Virginia Road, also of the Skelsmerdine family, and others, were members. Jack Liversage, a well known figure in Wallasey, also belonged to the club, which ultimately fell to pieces.

Another club called the "Lingfell", started in 1873, on land situated on the east side of Halstead Road, Somerville. It commenced in the following manner:- Four young men, Tom Hammer, Charlie Walmsley, James Owen and Dan McGrory, were talking one evening on the land where the Baths stand at Guinea Gap. The conversation turned on the absence of a cricket club in Seacombe or Egremont, and there and then it was decided to create one. Tom Hammer was elected captain. In 1876 the ground was required for building purposes, and that was the end of the club. Fortunately a Mr. Martin had come to live in 'Winch House' (now the site of Edith, Ethel and Florence Roads) and under his inspiration a new club was started. Many of the Lingfell players formed up again, which was called Egremont C.C. Later, about 1880, the New Brighton Club was in a bad way, and as Egremont's land was also to be built on, Mr. T.E. Edwards induced most of the best players to join New Brighton and the land in Rake Lane having been obtained.

WALLASEY IN THE 1930'S

Ever Changing

The 1930's in Wallasey were a strange mixture. Nothing like what had gone before. Nothing like anything that was to come. The decade opened with long summers and big plans. It closed with the wail of air-raid sirens and the drawing of black-out curtains.

The Thirties brought big extensions to the Promenade – and talk of the town becoming "Britain's premier garden city by the sea". It never did, but in the optimism of the time it seemed possible.

Wallasey was full of ideas. It was anxious to establish its north end as "a holidaymakers" playground.

New terminal at Seacombe Ferry, 1933

Older residents rubbed their eyes a lot in this decade.
Great changes took place. Development was rapid.
Hundreds more Council houses sprang up. There were important extensions to all the public services.
Things moved quickly. There was something happening all the time.
There were years of publicity stunts and public works. Big and confident, Wallasey was going places.
Seacombe Ferry got its clock tower in 1932. A year later the whole ferry entrance – "gateway to the town" – was re-built.
The Lyceum Cinema, formerly on the site of the Apollo Six Cinema, King Street (and originally a Presbyterian Church) went up in flames in December, 1931. The Gaumont rose from the ashes two years later.
Lieut-Col. Moore-Brabazon was M.P. Election campaigns were big and noisy. No holds barred.

Construction of the Derby Pool, 1932

In 1932 they opened the Derby Pool. In 1934 they opened the New Brighton Pool – then one of the largest in the world.

Swimming was a big sport of the era. Most of the champions came to town.

The Duke of Windsor, then Prince of Wales, visited the Mariners' Home, Seabank Road, on 4th November, 1931. A few years later he was to be caught up in the constitutional crisis that rocked the country.

Wallasey hit the national headlines in 1932. The tanker 'British Commando' wrecked part of Egremont Ferry in the May. The last tramcars ran on 1st December, 1933. In the same year New Brighton got its £95,000 Marine Lake. Wallasey Grammar got public school status.

Central Park Playground, August 1939

Big extensions of the electricity services came. They built more schools – Gorsedale, Barnston Lane, and the 'Central School', at New Brighton.

In the cinemas the newsreels were full of the exploits of people like aviator Amy Johnson, Capt. Malcolm Campbell, with his racing car 'Blue Bird', and tennis players Helen Wills Moody and Fred Perry.

Hundreds of Wallasey people joined a public walk through the newly-completed Mersey Tunnel in July, 1934. There were street parties in 1935 for the Silver Jubilee of King George V.

After the death of George V early in 1936, followed by the abdication of King Edward VIII, the Coronation of George VI in May, 1937, was a time for local school children at New Brighton Pool. There were street parties. There was a mammoth display of physical training by local school children at New Brighton Pool.

*Street party for the coronation of George
VI, Hawthorne Grove, 1937*

Fairy-lights and illuminated buses. Presents of tins of chocolates and books for the youngsters.
There were carnival processions and fireworks and displays. There were patriotic concerts and big parades.

Dole Queues

But if there were bright and happy moments, there were also many dark days of trouble. Trade depression brought unemployment figures to a high level.
There were long queues outside the Labour Exchange in Seacombe. There were angry political demonstrations.
A 'Poor Kiddies Clothing Fund' was opened by the Police. Hundreds of boys and girls were issued with boots, warm jerseys and

frocks.

There were things called 'Poor Kiddies Outings'. There were Christmas issues of 'goodies' for families who might otherwise have had nothing to celebrate with. Notices declaring that there were 'No Vacancies' were a common sight outside factories and in shop windows. Life was for too many a hard, fierce struggle.

Things started to get better in the last couple of years of the decade. The 'Blue Skies' of the song seemed to be coming. Jobs became more plentiful.

"Happy Days Are Here Again", sang the radio crooners. It rather looked as if they might have something.

Coronation Buildings, Wallasey Road, Liscard, 1938

More people began to have more money – enough of it to buy at least some of the good things.

There was plenty to spend the money on. The shops were packed.

At "the pictures" there was Fred Astaire and Ginger Rogers, Dick Powell, "Our Gang", Tom Walls, and Robert Donat.

Shirely Temple ("On The Good Ship Lollipop"), the Dead End Kids, Gracie Fields, Anna May Wong, and John Boles.

Sonja Henie, Don Ameche, Carole Lombard, Jane Withers, Dolores Del Rio, Mickey Rooney and Judy Garland in the "Andy Hardy" comedies.

Everything cheap.

There were plenty of houses to let in the town. You could get

one in Kingsway for 17s. 6d a week.
There were plenty of houses for sale. You could buy one in Radnor Drive (5 bedroom) for £400.
Coal was 30s. a ton. Scotch was 12s. 6d. a bottle. Cigarettes a shilling for twenty.
Housewives were buying tea at 1s. 9d. a pound. Butter was tenpence a pound.
Eggs a penny each. A man suit for £1.
A three-piece suite cost about £8. You could get a leg of lamb for about 3s.

War Approaches

Despite uneasy years of warnings, and rumblings in Europe, there were those who couldn't believe it couldn't last. It seemed so safe and sure.
Up at the Tower Ballroom, to the music of the Playboys Band, the young people were boomps-a-daisying-it at the 1s. 6d. Saturday night hops.
Frank Terry had his "New Brighton Follies" at the Floral Pavilion.
People like Emlyn Williams, 'Hutch', and Yvonne Arnaud were appearing at the Winter Gardens.
Then, in 1939, towards the end of a bumper summer season, another war wrote another full stop in the story of the town's development.
A party of German schoolboys were visiting the town. Their headmaster wrote to Wallasey Grammar School: "Whenever there is any hope left it is in youth".
Late in August, 1939 saw the evacuation of thousands of Wallasey schoolchildren. They left Seacombe Station in special trains.
Everyone was issued with a gas mask. Reservists were reporting to military depots.
Identity cards. "Watch that light!" Tin hats. The A.R.P.
On 3rd September, a quiet Sunday, crowds at New Brighton

gathered outside shops and cafes to hear Prime Minister Chamberlain's speech on the radio.

The local paper observed the following week that "after the announcement of war the town seemed to go very still. It was as though a great quiet was spreading over the place". The years which began with pierrots on the pier ended with black-out curtains on every window. The Town Hall got a cocoon of sandbags. There were barrage balloons in the parks. Wallasey, like the world outside, was never going to be the same again.

WALLASEY FERRYBOATS THAT SAILED OFF TO WAR

The Iris and Daffodil were the twin sisters of the Wallasey Ferries that took an excursion into hell and came back glorious. They sailed off to war in naval grey, with an H.M.S. before their names. They took part in one of the great exploits in naval history. They limped home battle-scarred, and were awarded the designation 'Royal'. From the quiet daily round of ferrying passengers across the Mersey, they went into the shells and minefields of 'the first commando raid of all' – and helped write a chapter in the story of World War One.

The 'Iris' and Daffodil', twin-screw steamers, were built in 1906. The 'Iris' was 491 tons, the 'Daffodil' 482. Both were just over

159 feet in length.

They were the first vessels in the ferry fleet to sport a flying bridge and a promenade deck extending the full width of the ship.

Handsome-looking, they were an improvement on all that had gone before, with their three separate saloons on deck, with their graceful lines. For twelve years they ferried to and from Seacombe. A quiet, uneventful job.

"'Iris' and 'Daffodil' return at dawn from Zeebrugge after the fight", was the title of this painting done locally in 1918. They are shown steaming back to Dover.

They encountered nothing more dangerous than Mersey fogs. They became familiar, friendly sights.

Then, towards the end of World War One, they were taken over by the Admiralty. They were 'called up', like so many men from the town to which they belonged.

They were painted grey. They were manned by the Royal Navy. They went to war.

The Germans had occupied Zeebrugge, on the Belgian coast, in 1914. Owing to the wishes of the British Army, the mole and harbour works there were not destroyed by the British Navy before it withdrew.

It became a German submarine and destroyer base of the most formidable character. Immense concrete shelters gave a large measure of security.

The object of the British attack in 1918 was to block the Bruges Canal at its entrance into Zeebrugge Harbour. This was to be effected by sinking three old cruisers filled with cement.

As the cruisers had to pass batteries on the mole, it was first necessary to destroy the batteries.

The vessels chosen to carry the troops for this attack were the cruiser 'Vindictive' and the ferryboats 'Iris' and 'Daffodil' – which drew only eight feet six inches of water and therefore could be safety taken over minefields.

The night of April 22/23 was heavy and overcast when the naval force went into action under Vice-Admiral Keyes.

The 'Vindictive', commanded by Commander A.F.B. Carpenter, ran in, protected by smoke screens, through a storm of shells to the mole, with the 'Iris' and the 'Daffodil'.

On reaching the mole at Zeebrugge the 'Vindictive's' anchors failed to hold, and the captain of the 'Daffodil', although wounded, pinned the 'Vindictive' to the mole by manoeuvring into position against her.

The 'Vindictive's' gangway were dropped, and the landing parties stormed across them. In order to keep in position, an enormous head of pressure had to be maintained in the 'Daffodil's' boilers.

It was a strenuous effort for her engines. At one point the engine room was holed and two compartments flooded.

Meanwhile, the 'Iris' was making an unsuccessful attempt to land her troops. The scaling ladders would not hold.

Her captain decided to land his troops vis the 'Vindictive'. But no sooner was his ship in position alongside her than the 'Daffodil' sounded the retirement, showing that the operation was complete.

The 'Iris', to the bitter disappointment of all on board, was instructed to cast off and make her way home.

Turning away northwards, the ferryboat came within range of

the shore batteries and received hits which smashed the port side of her bridge and left her conning positions on fire.

She was by now well off course. Again and again she was hit by gunfire.

Shells crashed through her sides and swept her decks. Her casualty figures rocketed from three to one hundred and fifty in a few minutes.

A single big shell plunged through the upper deck of the 'Iris'. It burst below at a point where fifty-six Marines were waiting. Forty-nine of them were killed and the remaining seven severely wounded.

Another shell in the ward room, which was serving as a sick bay, killed four officers and twenty-six men.

The ferryboat limped on. The only thing which saved her was that Lieutenant G. Spencer, her navigating officer, badly wounded, had managed to correct her course in the split second before the shell landed. As the helm swung over, the 'Iris' answered.

She was able to set off her damaged smoke canisters and retire behind her own smoke screen, but not before three more shells from the heavy shore batteries had found their target.

Desperately crippled, with an appalling loss of life, a fire raging below her bridge, and with flooding in her forward compartments, she struggled home to Dover.

At Dover she found her sister ship, 'Daffodil', had been towed there by another vessel, the 'Trident'.

In a message to Wallasey immediately after the action, Vice-Admiral Keyes said: "Your two stout vessels carried blue-jackets and Marines to Zeebrugge and remained alongside the mole for an hour, greatly contributing to the success of the operation.

"They will return to you directly the damage caused by the enemy's gunfire has been repaired..."

Proudly reporting the role of the local vessels in the raid, the local news reported; "They said the accustomed paths of peace and ventured forth valiantly to face the dread perils of war.

Battle-scarred, the 'Iris' at anchor in the Mersey on May 17th, 1918, with bluejackets aboard her.

"Wallasey, England's youngest borough, has now an opportunity to put on record her share in the story of a great battle..."
The newspapers described the attack as "brilliant", and the conduct of the two ferryboats from the Mersey as "gallant" in the extreme".
The battle-scarred vessels sailed home to Wallasey on May 17th, 1918. The Mersey gave them a welcome fit for heroes.
Lifeboat rockets were fired from New Brighton as they dropped anchor off New Brighton Pier. The promenade was packed with sightseers.
Tram-cars were decorated for the occasion. Flags flew from every building.
A band played. Ships blazed their sirens in salute.
Officers and men were greeted by the Mayor, Alderman F.F.Scott, at Egremont.
The Mayoress was presented with a huge bunch of irises and daffodils by Lieutenant Stansfield, the only officer of the 'Iris' to survive the action.
For two days both vessels were berthed at Canning Dock. Thousands of people visited them there.

For their heroic service the ferryboats were given the designation 'Royal'.

The shrapnel-ridden funnel of the 'Iris' stood for many years on the south side of Seacombe Ferry as a memorial. Her bell hung in the ferry vestibule for many years. The bell now stands proudly outside Earlston Reference Library. For years they continued to serve the ferries. Then, in 1931, the 'Royal Iris' was brought for use as a cruise steamer at Dublin. In 1933 the 'Royal Daffodil' was sold to the Medway Steam Packet Company. After several years' service on the Thames she was sold for scrap. Eventually, the 'Royal Iris' went to Cork Harbour and was renamed 'Blarney'. She was broken up in 1938 From the 1920's a commemorative service had been held aboard a Wallasey ferryboat on the Sunday nearest to St. George's Day. Survivors of the action use to travel to Wallasey for the occasion.

After their return from Zeebrugge, the two vessels were put on public show in Liverpool before their damage was repaired. Visitors view the promenade deck of Iris. Note the damaged bridge and the wreath in tribute to the fallen.

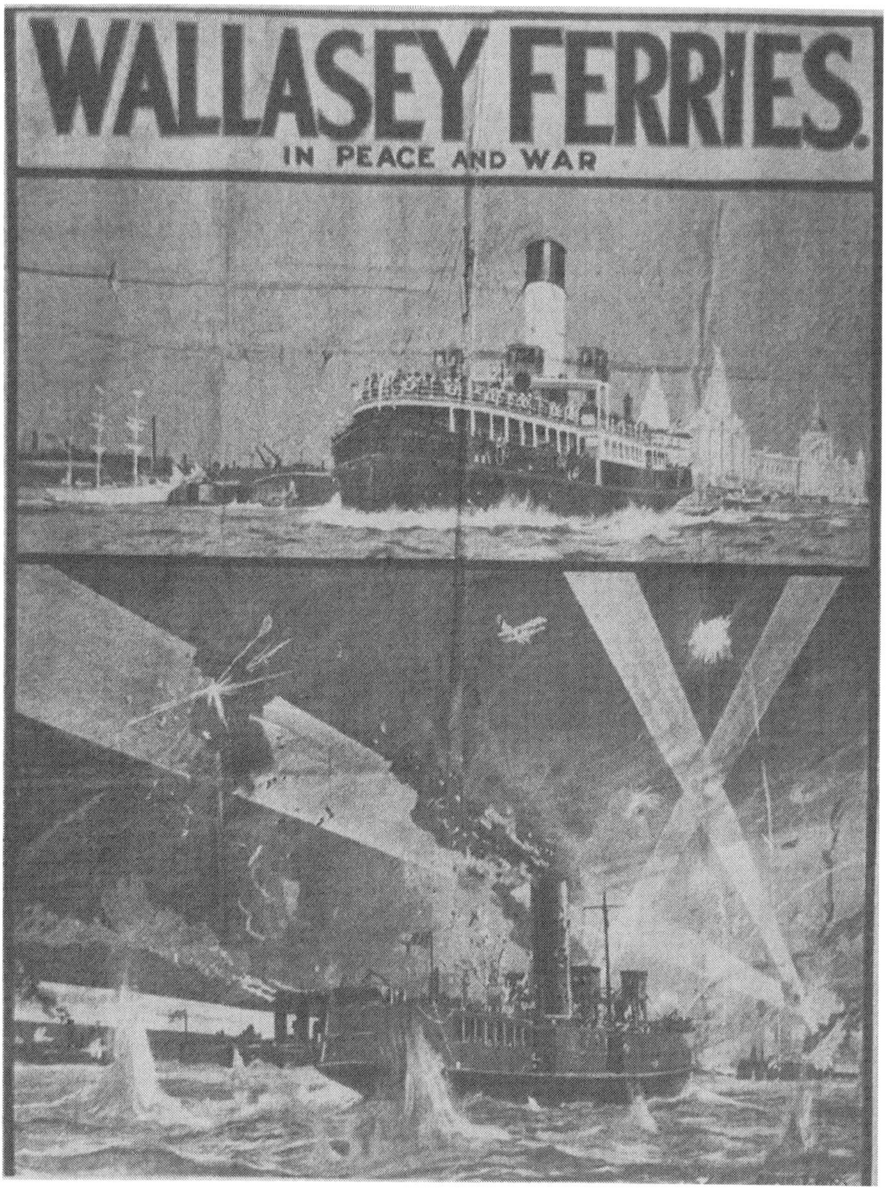
WALLASEY FERRIES.
IN PEACE AND WAR

LISCARD & THE MONKEY HOUSE

Liscard established itself as a place to shop over 150 years ago when its neighbours of Egremont, Seacombe and Wallasey Village, were little more than clusters of cottages and pocket-sized industries.

Liscard then extended from the vicinity of the Queen's Arms to the corner of Seaview Road. A section of Seaview Road was guarded by a high brick wall. It stretched from the Wellington Hotel to about Seaview Avenue, and it was adorned at one point with a drinking fountain in the shape of a large shell.

Running behind Victoria Central Hospital and across Oxton Road is Love Lane. It was often referred to as Cuffy Lane, for near it was a field called Cuff Hey.

At the Liscard end of the lane, which is now Greenheys Road, was a wooden stile; a stone stile was situated at Pemberton's

Cottage, near Leominster Road, and a third, also a wooden one, at the Poulton end of the lane.

At the turn of the 20th Century a right of way still existed from Liscard Road to Martin's Lane which passed through the grounds of Liscard House. Nearby, under a stone trough dark opening of a dried-up well, round which clung legends of a Cromwellian soldier who sought a hiding place. It was reputed to be nearly 200 feet deep.

They named Monk Road and Newell Road in honour of Mr Thomas Monk and his son-in-law and partner, John Newell, the constructors of the Great Float Docks and the Seacombe Ferry approaches.

Liscard Castle, Seaview Road

Longview Avenue and Newland Drive both took the names of old houses, and Urmson Road, formerly Townfield Lane, was named after an old Liscard family. Rake Lane's origin is interesting. 'Rake' means lane, and so the highway is virtually called Lane Lane.

Sir John Tobin built the fine old manor house that was in Central Park. Later it became School of Art but after a fire it was demolished in 2008. It was surrounded by the fields and garden which now form Central Park.

Another big house in the district was Liscard Castle. The title is misleading. It never was a castle, although its battlements and stone lion embellishments have it a certain dignity. The house was built in 1841 and surrounded by trees. It was occupied by a brush manufacturer, John Marsden. Later the house was converted into three residences: the Turrets, the Towers and the Castle. Roads bearing two of these names now mark the site. The house stood til 1902 when it was demolished. The locals called it Marsden Folly.

Standing on the corner of Rake Lane and Liscard Village was Mona Cottage. it stood almost opposite the Post Office. It was sometimes caled the Oyster Cottage, for its window mullions were covered with shells.

There was Egerton Cottage, There was Cruck's Cottage. There was Granny Smith's, in Mill Lane, and Ivy Cottage, Liscard Road. An interesting little block of houses in Liscard Village known as Dean Terrace and dates back to 1782. This would seem to be one of the earliest local attempts to construct a few dwellings designed in terrace form.

Others slightly later are Littler's Terrace, at the end of which is the old King's Arms Hotel, Liscard Road, and Springfield Terrace, at the eastern of Martin's Lane.

Up to the early 1920's Mill Lane really had a mill pond. On its bank stood a farm. The site is now occupied by Eldon Road.

The old Boot Inn was the favourite local. The building, quaint and irregular is detailed in the next chapter.

The first elementary school opened in Liscard was in a building in Liscard Road. It still stands today, almost opposite the ambulance station. The school was connected with St. John's Church until the 1980's, when it became St. Mary's Boys School. It was closed shortly after the Great War. St. Mary's Girls' School was further along the road. It was on a site that later became Marks & Spencers and other shops.

The old Wellington Hotel jutted out into Wallasey Road. It was demolished to make way for the new building in the 1930s. Today it's called Dukes.

Monkey House, on the left, Liscard Village. 1924

After the Great War Liscard became really busy. Sadly during the 1920's and 1930's the last of the old cottages went. In came the big stores. Modern fittings replaced the old slabs and open windows. Down tumbled the 'Monkey House', the pagoda-like-public shelter which stood where the traffic lights of the one-way system is today at the junctions of Seaview Road, Wallasey Road and Liscard Road. Underneath it were public conveniences. Tramcars stopped at it. It was a popular meeting place. The shelter was removed in 1926. The conveniences stayed until the 1930's.

Liscard radically changed from the 1960's. Road widened, one-way traffic system introduced, houses demolished to make way for an improved and established shopping precinct.

P. DAVIES

Rossett Place, Liscard, 1939. Liscard Water Tower can be seen on Mill Lane. The houses were demolished by the 1960's to make way for the shopping precinct and a car park

St. Alban's Terrace, 1960's, spire of St. Alban's church can be seen in the distance. The houses were demolished to make way for the Cherry Tree shopping precinct..

1914

SHOPPING IN LISCARD: PICTORIAL

A look round old Liscard Town Centre.

Different views over the years of Panter Bricks shoe shop: 1900, 1928 and 1976. Once stood on the corner of Liscard Road and Mill Lane. The shop was demolished to make way for road widening.

P. DAVIES

Wallasey Road, 1936, with St. Alban's Road to the immediate right. The old Wellington Pub stands centre top.

A VIEW FROM THE TOWER

Wallasey Road with Moseley Avenue on the left, c1930's,

Birkenhead Co-Operative Store, Liscard Road, 1966

Birkenhead Co-Operative Store, 1st Floor Fashion, 1966

Gear Box, 144 Seaview Road, 1968
Clarendon Furnishings, Wallaset Road, 1967

View from the roundabout looking down Liscard Road, 1968

View of Wallasey Road looking towards the Boot Inn, 1968

Cherry Tree Town Centre, 1970's

LAST ORDERS PLEASE!

The Sebastopol, the Jolly Sailor, the Blue Bell, The Long Pull, The Abbottsford. Pubs of a long ago. They served their 'last orders' more than a lifetime ago.

For its size, Wallasey has always been well provided with pubs. By the 1960's the population of the Borough was 104,000 and there was sixty pubs. In them, the mahogany and leaded glass fixtures had given way to thick carpets and dinky tables. They were bright, upholstered pubs. Today's pubs are themed or offer a varied cuisine. Pubs of long ago were open practically twenty fours a day. They started serving at 6 am. They closed whenever the last customer left.

Old Pool Inn and Pinfold, c1842

Ring O'Bells, Wallasey Village, c1948

Black Horse, 1880's

Cheshire Cheese, c1880

There is a document dated 1561 which contains "the names of

all p'sons which kept alehouses within the Hundred of Werroll."
Four were in Wallasey.
The old Cheshire Cheese, in Wallasey Village, was among them. So was the Boot Inn, Liscard, the Seacombe Boathouse, and the old Pool Inn, Poulton.
All in time demolished. Their successors have been erected on slightly different sites. The Seacombe Boathouse and Pool Inn passed out of existence.
The original Cheshire Cheese was white washed and thatched-roofed. An old drawing shows it to have had thick timbers and oak settlers. It stood amid fields, cottages and little farms, the parish church on the hill behind it. The narrow village street had hedges and lilac trees. It was said that King William of Orange slept at the Cheshire Cheese before he sailed for Ireland. The building was demolished in 1884. The present building dates from the 1890's. The old Pool Inn faced down Poulton Bridge Road, thus standing a little south of the one that replaced it. Although not dated, it was believed to go back to the seventeenth century. It was white-washed, with ornamental curved gables of the Dutch type. Near it stood a circular pinfold for cattle.
A stream ran past it from Mill Lane. Nearby was the village water pump. Both the building and the pump disappeared over a century ago. The building which had replaced the old Pool Inn was demolished in 2010.
A legend surrounds the Boot Inn. It is difficult to sift the actual fact from the fiction of the old place. The old Inn, taken down almost a century ago for road widening and to make room for the present premises, was known to have existed in Elizabethan times, but the house had been so altered and reconstructed over the years that few, if any, of the old features remained.
Up to about 1900 the Boot Inn was still a quaint, irregular building. The legend attached to its name ran roughly as follows:
One wild night in the reign of Good Queen Bess a fierce horseman galloped to its door. Upon being admitted, he produced a

great horse pistol and a big jack boot. The licensee and his wife overpowered him.

Then in bounded three gentlemen, one of whom had just been robbed of his jackboot by the horseman. The boot contained gold.

The licensee and his wife were given ten guineas apiece. The robber was given to the gibbet. "And the boot to be a sign untoe the inn while it doth stand."

The legend is preserved in a glass case at the new 'Boot'. So is the remarkable boot.

In 1924 work began on demolishing the old pub and the following year the new Boot Inn opened. In 1948 the car park was constructed. By 2004 the Boot changed its name to the Turnberry but changed it back in 2008 to the Boot.

Wallasey Village's Black Horse is believed to have taken its name from a horse entered in a race at Leasowe by Lord Molyneux in the 1700's. The original building stood until 1931. The interior was cosy, and the house a long one, with a cobbled frontage. At the corner was an old horse-mounting block. At the side was the village mortuary.

On the front wall of the modern building bears the name on the lintel stone initialled and dated D.W.M. 1722, with a saddle but into the stone.

The Albion, Albion Street, New Brighton, goes back nearly 200 years, opening in about 1835,. It was built by one of the Earls of Derby. Over its old gates were the arms of the House of Stanley. The building was largely altered over the years. The pub closed shortly after 2000 and converted to flats.

In Liscard, the Queen's Arms Hotel has the unusual distinction of having once been used as a magistrate's court. Local cases were heard there in the last years of the 19th century, before the town's first court house was built in Liscard Road (premises became the Continental and later demolished).

Another lost pub of yester-year was the Castle Hotel, Wallasey Road. The pub opened in 1887. It was also known as the 'Garden Inn'. The pub closed in 1964 to make way for the Cherry Tree

Centre.

Standing on St. Hilary's Brow was the high chimneyed building of the Sebastopol. It once stood at the Breck Road end, and was given its name after the taking of Sebastopol at the end of the Crimean War in 1855. The pub was demolished in 1930 for road widening.

Sebastopol, 1912

The Long Pull was in Tobin Street, Egremont and stood until the First World War. It got its name from the steep incline from the shore, an incline on which many a heavily-laden horse-drawn cart encountered difficulty.

In Limekiln Lane was the Jolly Sailor which was nothing more than a country cottage. It was a snug and friendly house with a lantern hung over the front door. The pub served mainly to sailors from the Birkenhead docks and closed in the 1920's.

The Abbottsford once stood on the corner of Borough Road and Demesne Street, which was demolished in the 1960's to make way for the block of flats, Mersey Court. It was a popular local pub, with noisy Saturday nights.

Another very old pub of days gone by was the Blue Bell. It was a curious old place of uncertain date. It stood next to the old Fire Station in Liscard Village. Both demolished in time. The pub had a roof that was covered in turf. Over it grey a crop of grass. The building came down in the 1900's.

Popular with agricultural workers was the Ring O'Bells which stood on the corner of School Lane, in Wallasey Village. It dated back to at least 1860. The pub had a bar in a tiny room. By the 1900's the building became, first a dwelling, then later a small general store before being demolished in the 1950's for local development.

The Plough Inn was situated on Mount Pleasant Road and dates back to 1860 and closed in 1931. It once stood on the corner of a court yard.

There were three breweries in Wallasey. Spragg's Ales was the most popular local beers that were sold in the pubs. The brewery began in 1856 and stood in Leasowe Road and lasted some 50 years. The other two breweries, The Grosvenor, in Borough Road, Seacombe, operated from the 1840's until the 1890's and there was Dickenson's, in Hope Place, off Wallasey Road. Their horse-drawn heavily laden wagons were a familiar sight on the roads of Wallasey.

But the Long Pull, Jolly Sailor and the Sebastopol, as well as others, have all gone for ever. They once appeared in the old trade directories of the town. They are just names now, but in their time social centres. Meeting places for the community. For them, it is last ordes, please!

DAYS OF OUTINGS AND CELEBRATION

Wallasey use to be a great place for parades and processions as well as celebrations. Staging them was practically a local industry.

They had parades for royal jubilees, for wartime victories, for local anniversaries, and anything else they could make an excuse of. Workingmen's outings became popular in the years before the Great War. Nearly every pub and club in the town had its 'annual'.

In Sunday suits and check caps, the men went off into Wirral. The day would be devoted to bowling, betting and downing vast quantities of strong beer. They could get an ounce of tobacco for a few coppers, a packet of cigarettes for three pence, and a pint for twopence.

For the journey there was bottles of stout and beef sandwiches.

There was usually a hot-pot supper at the end. Sing-songs and shouts. Bellows of laughter, and occasional fights. Big, boisterous days. Plenty to eat, too much to drink.

Shaw Brothers horse and cart dressed up for a carnival, Liscard, 1905

For Wallasey, the days of over more than a century ago seemed full of rose days and pageants and fetes and carnivals. The town loved dressing up, getting out.
In fields along Poulton and Wallasey Village the locals put out tables filled with 'goodies'. Al fresco fun was quite the fashion. On Carnival days, tradesmen decorated carts. There was great rivalry.
Silver bands – nearly every district had its own – oomp-pah-oomp pahed parades through the streets. There was the Wallasey Village Festival. One of the big occasions in the local calendar. It had a great reputation.
There was also the poor kiddies' outings. There were outings for tramway employees and outings for ferrymen.
Later on, in the 1920's, Moreton organised the Donkey Derby. The local Catholic priest, Father Griffin, organised it, and famous jockeys of the time took part. Local charities did well out of all of it. It was a good thing they did, for calls on them were

heavy. There was unemployment. The poor was very poor indeed.

In the early years of the last century the 'treats' and picnics organised by the Sunday Schools were red letter days in the lives of local youngsters. Outings were rare things for boys and girls from modest homes. They were things to be looked forward to. Ferryboats were chartered. They took their young passengers up to Eastham, which then had a ferry and gardens. Each child was given a bag of sandwiches and cakes. Leasowe was also a favourite for the youngsters. Leasowe Road was a narrow winding lane with hedgerows of wild roses and honeysuckle. Oarside Farm, which stood at the bottom of Mount Pleasant Road, was one of the picnic sites the young children liked best.

The summer outings were the big occasions. Long tables laden with jam and cakes and biscuits. Ginger beer in old-type bottles and fizzy lemonade with real lemons. Sticky toffee in slabs, Liquorice in slender sticks. Chocolate in small tins.

They were days of simple, unsophisticated pleasure.

THE POTTER OF SEACOMBE

John Goodwin was the potter of Seacombe who sent the name of the town round the world. Today his wares are rare. His plates and sauces fetch collector's prices.

Goodwin came from Staffordshire in 1851 and established his factory down by the docks, just off Wheatland Lane. It was three storey high and had six kilns. The first oven was fire in 1852. Within a few months he had made his name. Colourful stoneware, decorated with country scenes, was being sold locally and shipped overseas.

The pottery attracted a great deal of attention. It was claimed to be the best built and equipped in England at that time.

The six kilns of the Seacombe Pottery, 1880's

The stoneware and earthenware was colour printed chiefly in a blue and purplish tint. Later Goodwin turned out some fine Parian ware.

John Goodwin died in 1857. He was buried in St. John's Churchyard, Egremont, just outside the railings by the entrance gate.

The pottery was taken over by Thomas Orton Goodwin, who lived in Wheatland Lane. He carried on for sixteen years.

Disaster struck in 1873 when a consignment of Seacombe pottery was lost at sea on the way to the American market. It was uninsured, and because of the resulting financial embarrassment, production ceased. The affair was the talk of the town at the time. The national newspapers were full of it.

Seacombe missed the pottery. It had provided jobs for a lot of people – and jobs were in short supply in the town of over 150 years ago. It was a landmark. Its products were held in high esteem.

Goodwin's enterprise was one of the first industries to come to

Wallasey. Up to his time agriculture, milling and brick-laying had been the only fields of employment for a growing population.

The Seacombe of 1851 was a place a real poverty. Two thirds of the population could neither read or write. Life was pretty wretched.

John Goodwin brought work and hope. He gave people something to do, something to take a pride in. He won their affection.

TOMBSTONES OF THE PAST

High on a hill in Wallasey Village is the church of St. Hilary's. In its churchyard are the weathered tombstones of our forefathers. They were once landed gentlemen and fine ladies as well as good and simple men and women who then tilled the fields of long ago and brought up families in little cottage homes.
We can bypass the history of St. Hilary's as it's been covered in an earlier chapter.
There is no evidence of graves of the earlier church. The earliest remains are from the 18th Century. The part of the churchyard around the old tower has been a burial ground for centuries. There are many old tombstones in it, but a few now bear readable inscriptions. There are, however, several stones which bear legible inscriptions recording burials over two centuries ago.
On either side of the old church is evidence of flat tombstones.

After the ruins of the church had been demolished, the site was used for burials, but by the time it had become common to erect vertical headstones on graves.

The old tower bears the date 1530 and has battlements, buttress, gargoyles and three-light belfry windows. Near it, on a raised marble tombstone, is the record of James Gordon, of Poulton-cum-Seacombe, who passed away in February, 1778, aged 82 years of age. There is also the body of his daughter Ann Smith, wife of Admiral Richard Smith. She died in July, 1779, aged 57 years of age.

Admiral Richard Smith built Rosebury House, which once stood on the north side of old School Lane, and was Lord of the Manor of Poulton in 1800. A squire in the old town, the admiral was paid a sum for vessels anchoring close to Poulton. The tombstone tells that he died on 26th January, 1811, aged 77 years old. On the same tombstone is the inscription: "Nathalie Gordon Smith, infant daughter of Henry Smith Esq., of this parish, who died on 26th Nov.1867, aged 14 days".

Near the gate that leads to Church Hill are three adjoining graves with the names of Gerald Stanley of Liscard who died in 1818, aged 80 years ("Possessed a sound mind, an honest heart"), and his wife Mary, who died in 1828, aged 83 years ("A pious and good Christian").

There is a memorial to the Stanley's two sons. It reads: "Sacred to the memory of Thomas Stanley, Eq., solicitor and notary public, native of this parish... who departed this life 14th April, 1822, at Port Louis, Isle of France, aged 40 years...

"Also of James Stanley, his brother, lieutenant of the 26th Regiment Native Infantry of the Hon. East India Company service, who died 20th November, 1822, at Calcutta, aged 32 years..."

To the east of the tower where the ground rises is the tombstone inscribed "Thomas Stewart Byrth, born October 5, 1837, died February 4, 1838, son of the Rev. Thomas Byrth and Mary his wife". Thomas was just five months old. His father, rector of St. Hilary's for 15 years, joined him in 1849, aged 56 years.

To the west of the old tower: "In memory of William Douglas, native of Dunfermline, Scotland, but for many years a citizen of New York, who was drowned near Leasowe Castle after leaving the wreck of the packet ship Pennsylvania during the memorable gale of January 8th, 1839..."

Mr. Douglas was aged 35. Close by lies Lucas B. Blydenburgh, of New York, mate of the Pennsylvania, who was drowned near Leasowe Castle, aged 40 years. Such names as Aynsdale, Rolin, Hesket, Pemberton, Smyth, Johnson, Robinson, Wilson and Byrd appear.

Epidemics in the area, such as cholera, can be judged from the number of people in one family who were buried within a few weeks of one another.

Entries in the burial section of the old parish registers regularly record drowning's at sea or in the Wallasey Pool. One records that two people were killed by the fall of a pinnacle. Murder was recorded too. Peter Watts, stranger to the parish, was done to death in 1695. Several "Welchmen shipwrecked and starved to death on Wallasey sand-hills..."

And, of course, all those short sad inscriptions of so-and-so at the age of a few days, a few months, or a year. The infantile mortality rate was pathetically high in those far off days. Big families lost many of their little ones. The ages at which they died, cut into the old stones in the St. Hilary's churchyard, reminds us of how easily death laid its hand on those who lived in harder times.

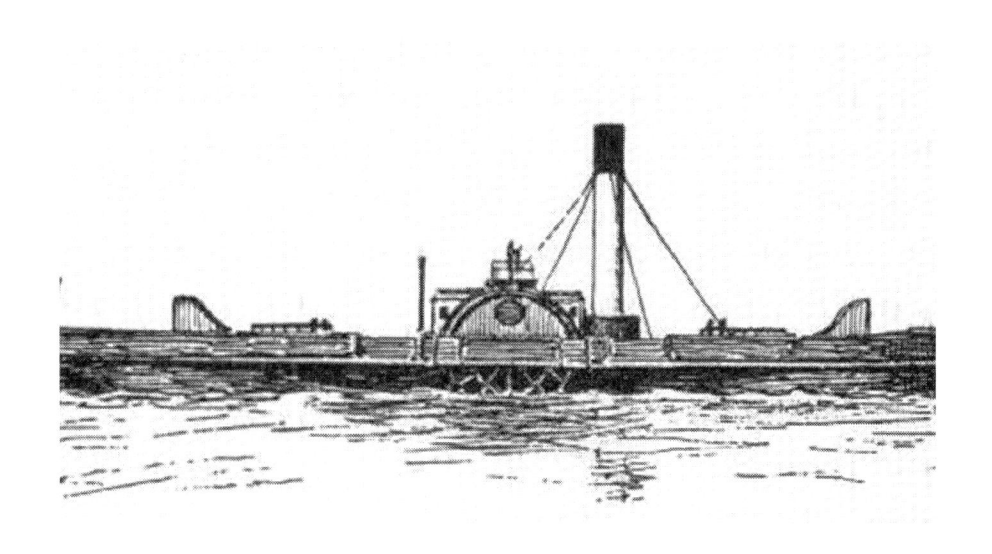

THE 'GEM' DISASTER

On Tuesday, 26th November 1878, one of the worst fogs in living memory covered the Mersey. Early on a cold morning, a small paddle-driven ferryboat cast off from Seacombe in the dense fog. A few minutes later it was in collision. There were screams and confusion. Panic ensued leading to drowning's.

For many years there had been complaints that pilots brought ships into the Mersey to an anchor in the direct ferry track between Seacombe and Liverpool. Harold Littledale, who resided at Liscard Hall, Central Park, made fervent protests to the Dock Board. The complaints were largely ignored but many people warned that sooner or later, a serious collision would be the result.

The day before, the sailing ship *'Bowfell'*, owned by Brocklebank's, had arrived in the river from Calcutta. She had been brought to anchor a little to the west of mid-river, between Alfred Dock and Seacombe Stage.

The morning broke with a thick fog. It was so dense that old stagers on the river said they had never seen one like it. The *'Gem'* left Seacombe but she should have departed at nine o'clock but she was delayed for thirty minutes.

The *'Gem'* was a 150 tonner, 133 foot long ferryboat that had been in service for about sixteen years. She was built by W. Allsup & Sons, of Preston, and was originally named *'Liscard'*. She had no saloons, only cabins below deck. That morning she was carrying 250 passengers. They were mainly business and office people on their way to work.

She was in charge of Captain William Cartwright. He was an experience master of 27 years and a member of an old local family. A few minutes after the vessel had left Seacombe contrary shouts were heard from the fore. "Go ahead", "Go astern", Go to starboard", and "Go to port". Suddenly, the *'Bowfell'* loomed from the darkness. Before the engines could be reversed, the *'Gem'* crashed sideways into her, just forward of the starboard sponson. As she swung on, she fell across the clipper bow of the *'Bowfell'*, the bowsprit of which carried away the bulwarks. The *'Gem's'* tall funnel crashed down amongst the passengers. In its fall the funnel severed the leg of one of the passengers, James Hodgkins, a clerk. He bled to death in a matter of minutes.

There was panic and screams. Cries of 'She's sinking'. There was a rush to the sides. One of the passengers rushed on to the bridge. He was ordered down by the skipper, who eventually seized him by the throat and threw him below.

Captain Cartwright called to the passengers to keep still, to remain calm. His voice could hardly be heard.

The *'Gem's'* boat was lowered into the water by some of the passengers. Twenty of thirty people jumped into it and threatened to swamp it. Seventeen of the passengers were able to clamber up the chains of the *'Bowfell'* or were helped by ropes flung to them by the ship's crew. On the *'Gem'* the passengers huddled in corners of the deck or peered through the fog in hope of rescue. In order to appease the passengers, two crew members went into the stokehold and cheerily announced "she's as dry as a bone." As it turned out, they were right.

After an hour or so the *'Gem'* left the side of the *'Bowfell'*. It was discovered then that she was not damaged below the waterline and had not been in any danger of sinking.

Captain Cartwright brought the vessel safely to the Birkenhead cattle stage. There were cheers from those on board.

The exact loss of life was never known, but it was believed that at least fifteen people were drowned. Many were badly injured.

The news of the collision shook the whole country. Local papers had their front pages edged in black. There were special services in all the local churches.

Shortly after the disaster, the *'Gem'* was sold out of the service. She went to a firm in West Africa. Whilst en-route to take up duties as a tender, she called at the Scilly Isles to replenish her bunkers. She parted her anchor cable during a storm, was driven ashore, and became a total wreck.

The *'Gem'* disaster had a far-reaching effect. Immediately after it, larger vessels were ordered. There was a new departure in ferryboat design. They brought in the *'Daisy'* and *'Primrose'*, with accommodation for over 900 passengers, with hulls divided into about a dozen watertight compartments – in case of collision.

There was more outcomes of the *'Gem'* tragedy. William Carson, the manager of the ferries, resigned, ferry services slumped, house prices fell because no one wanted to travel to and from Wallasey and the building trade went into recession as new houses in Wallasey were not being built. It was not until the opening of the new Seacombe terminal two years later that saw the ferries once again become popular for travellers.

TIVOLI THEATRE

New Brighton   Phone: Wallasey 1874

WEEK COMMENCING MONDAY, 17th, JANUARY, 1955
6-30   —   TWICE NIGHTLY   —   8-40
FOR ONE WEEK ONLY

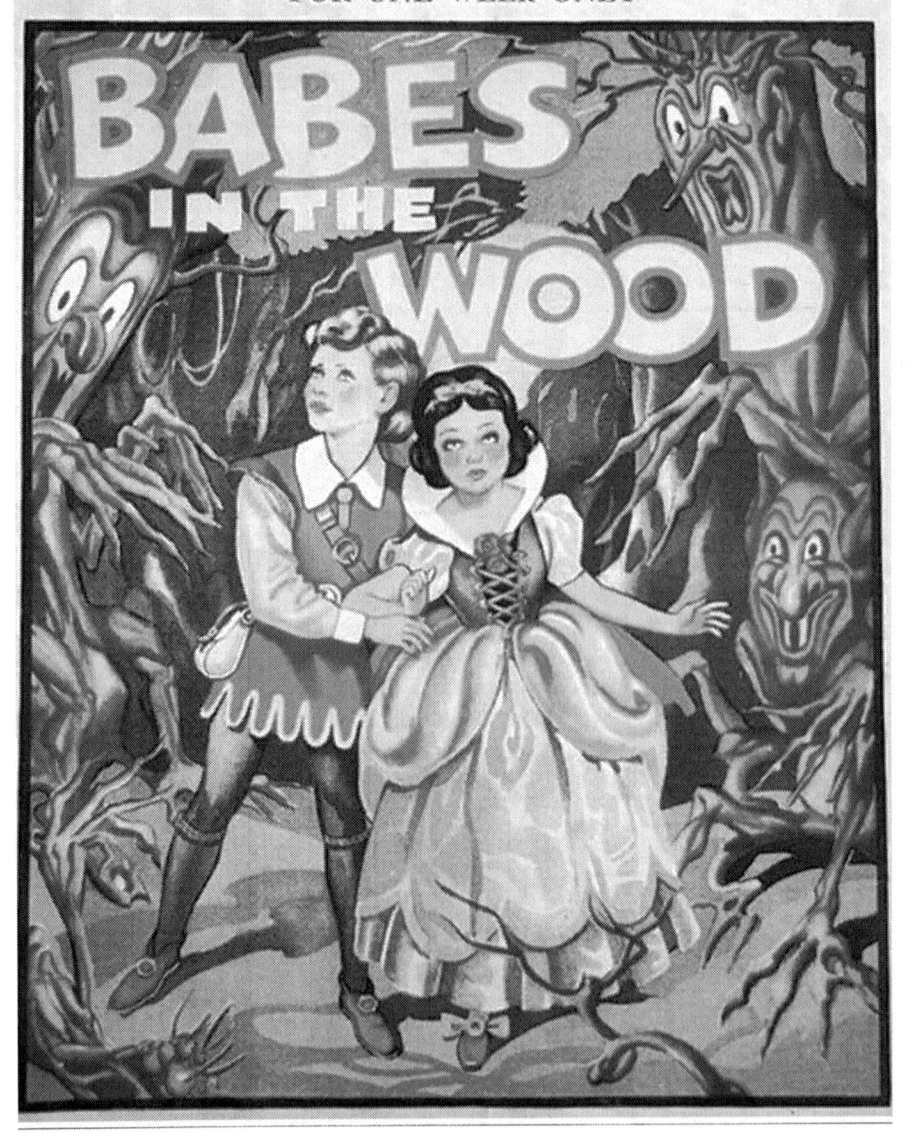

BABES IN THE WOOD

THE PROMENADE

Until 1891 the Mersey frontage was largely open to the Wallasey shore, with the exception of small areas adjoining the Seacombe ferries and the Ham and Egg Parade near New Brighton ferry. The building era was accelerated by the opening of the Mersey Railway in 1886 and of the connecting line to New Brighton in 1888, followed by the Seacombe branch in 1895.

The first length of promenade to be constructed was in 1891 between Egremont and Holland Road. In 1897 saw it extended to a point just beyond New Brighton Pier. In 1901 the portion between Egremont and Seacombe was built. Between 1906 and 1908 there were extensions from the Pier to the western boundary of Marine Park – a development which saw the demolishing of the notorious 'Ham and Egg' parade.

The acquisition of the river frontage from private land owners was also accompanied by successful efforts to secure as much as possible of the immediate background, in the interests of appearance and future control.

As a result of the land purchases there came into being Riverside School, Guinea Gap Baths, the Town Hall, Vale Park, the Tower Grounds and so on. These plans excited great publicity. A massive sea wall, a promenade 130 feet wide, with 46 acres of public gardens, a marine lake of 10 acres, a huge open-air bathing pool, and approach roads.

In the late 1920's, when thousands of men on Merseyside were out of work, the Unemployment Grants Committee approved the scheme for grant purposes. Work on extending the promenade as far as the Red Noses began at the cost of £531,000. Work on the remainder of the promenade, to Harrison Drive, was completed in 1939. The Second World War and its aftermath prevented the scheme going any further, maybe to West Kirby.

PROMENADE CONSTRUCTION : PICTORIAL

1931/1932

Promenade construction in front of Victoria Gardens, 1931

Constructing the slipway on the Promenade.
Centre top is the New Brighton Pier, 1931

Promenade Extension, July 1931

Driving steel sheet piling piling on the man wall, March 1932

Constructing the Marine Lake, 1932

STORMY WEATHER

Our weather always seems to hit the headlines. Storms have hit Wallasey on a number of occasions - the storm of 1990 would be considered by many the most destructive. On the night of Thursday, 26th February 1903 a destructive gale swept across Wallasey, Liverpool and surrounding district. That night the gale was accompanied with torrential rain and vivid flashes of lightening. The morning revealed a scene of desolation, many chimneys having been blown down, trees uprooted, huge advertising boards overthrown, shop windows smashed, and houses unroofed.

In one incident Miss Lizzie Pollard, of 58 Buchanan Road, Seacombe and Mr. Walter Howden, of 9 Massey Park, Liscard, were proceeding to Seacombe Ferry, with the intention of crossing to Liverpool, when, as they passed opposite the Seacombe Railway Station, the boardings at that point were blown down, and fell on the unfortunate couple. Both were taken to Victoria Central

Hospital by ambulance and on arrival they were examined and it was found they both were severely bruised and shaken.

Poulton felt the full force owing to the exposed area. Many tiles were stripped from many buildings, and windows broken. The row of shops near Winterhey Avenue felt the full force of the hurricane. One shop had the tiles torn clean off, while the boundary wall at the rear was demolished. Considerable damage was done to the American Steam Laundry, Poulton Road, the roof of the coach house being lifted completely off the building and deposited in the yard.

Storm damage at the Open Air Bathing Pool, Feb 1990

The extensive hoardings between Albemarle Road and Brougham Road were completely destroyed, and large portions of the woodwork were blown into Hood Street.

The windows of the Rake Lane Schools, Liscard, were so badly damaged that the children had to be sent home.

Further damage was done to the greenhouses of the Wallasey market gardners and the plate-glass windows in Boots' chemist shop, King Street, was smashed by the wind.

A large chimney stack on a house at the top of Falkland Road, was blown down on Thursday night, and crashed through the roof, doing considerable damage.

A much earlier storm struck the parish on the 7th and 8th January 1839 and was described as "terror-stricken". Many small boats out on the Mersey were pounded against each other or against the sea walls and sunk in the fury of the storm. Many lives were lost, including women and children, on board the packet ships *Pennsylvania* and *Lockwoods*. The *Lockwoods* was an emigrant ship with 108 souls on board, most of whom were drowned. The steam tug *Victoria* towed out the lifeboat, which was housed at the Magazines (Lane). After several journeys the tug and lifeboat saved 55 people from the *Lockwoods* (including a baby which had been born a couple of days before). Many of the drowned are buried at St. Hilary Churchyard. Some are corded in an earlier chapter - Tombstones of the Past. As soon as the hurricane abated the locals began to plunder the wrecks.

The hurricane caused much damage to the parish. Slates blew off the roofs, bricks and coping stones flew "like hailstones" and walls and even the sides of houses collapsed. Dozens of heavy chimney stacks crashed through the roofs of houses, carrying bedroom and ground floors into the basements and caused the deaths of many people who were in bed or sheltering in the lower parts of houses.

FIRST WALLASEY BATHS?

Question - Where was Wallasey's first open air public baths? Wallasey's first public baths was not actually the New Brighton Open Air Pool or even Derby Pool. In fact it was located at one time at the foot of Wheatland Lane, Birkenhead Road end. The old Bee Hotel use to be on the opposite side until it was demolished to make way for the docks. The tide used to come close up to it and an old sailing vessel was anchored there. The sea water was allowed to flow into it, and this was the original sea water bath of Wallasey!

IN AND AROUND OLD WALLASEY

The Story Behind The Old Pictures

May Day Parade in Brighton Street, 1894.

The above image was taken from the bottom of Falkalnd Road, looking towards Seacombe on Brighton Street. Harrowby Road is on the left, between the block of shops. In the far distance on the left, fronted by a clump of trees, is North Meade estate, now the site of the Town Hall.

On March 25th, 1914 the foundation stone of the Town Hall was laid by King George V. Forty thousand people watched in Central Park as the King, accompanied by Queen Mary, pressed a lever and 'let loose' an electric current that laid the foundation stone for the Town Hall. When the First World War broke out it was used as a military hospital. The building was not opened for municipal purposes until 3rd November, 1920.

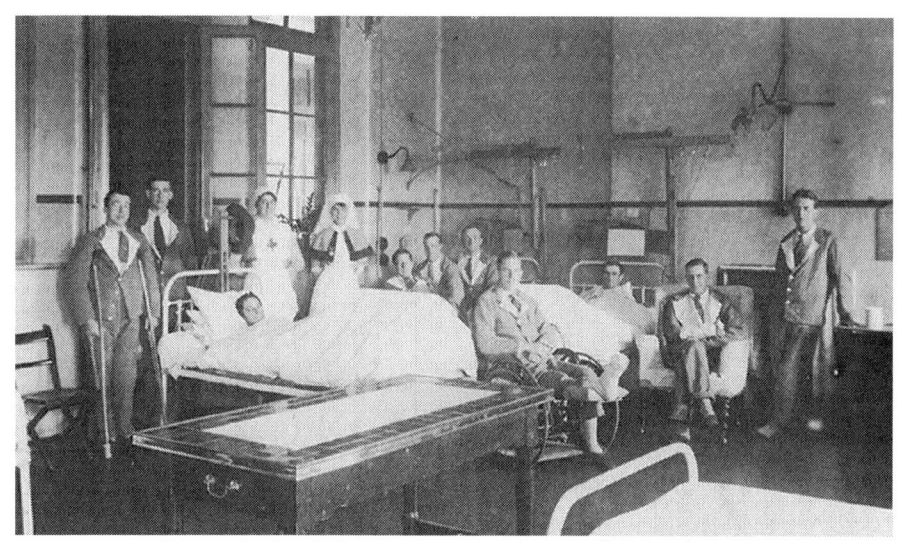

*Wounded soldiers recuperating at the Wallasey
Town Hall during the Great War*

Capitol Cinema, Liscard, 1927.
Originally the site on the corner of Liscard Village and Seaview

Road was Gibson Corner stable yards.

The Capitol Cinema opened on Saturday, 4th September 1926 and closed in 1974. The building was not used again until converted for bingo as well as a social club in 1978. It remained so until the early 1990s when it again closed.

Flats and maisonettes now cover the site of the old police station (image above) at the ferry end of Church Road in Seacombe. This picture was taken over a hundred years ago

Behind it lay old Seacombe Railway Station. Some years after this picture was taken a pet shop opened on the land next door to it. The station and the shop disappeared in the late 1950's.

With it leaded windows and mellow bricks, the 'cop shop', as many called it, had the appearance of a picturesque country house. There was always a policeman in residence.

The next image (top right) is Grove Road c1914, when the ladies wore long skirts and tram-lines criss-crossed the town. In the centre two boys are pushing a bread delivery cart. The picture was taken from Wallasey Village end. To the edge is the old Grove Hotel. Melody Inn Club occupied part of it. The building was later demolished.

St. Mary's School in the above picture was in Liscard Road. The building, greatly altered and modernised for business premises, still stands today almost opposite the ambulance station. This picture was taken almost a hundred years ago. It shows all the boys of the school lined up outside.

An aerial view of North Liscard. Pinpointed about the centre of the picture was the Grammar School and the Technical College. To the left is Rake Lake Cemetery. River Mersey at the top of the image.

Next is a mid-20th-Century sketch view of the Floral Pavilion Theatre. It opened in 1913 and replaced the eye-sore Ham and Egg Parade. Advertised outside the theatre is the Melody Inn which ran from 1948 to 1973. As part of redevelopment on the New Brighton promenade the Floral Pavilion was demolished in 2006 and a new £12 million 800 plus seat theatre and Conference Centre was built.

Liscard shopping precinct as we know today has radically changed over the past 50 years. So much has changed. St. Mary's school, pictured above, was purchased by Mr. J.Boughey and Mr. Leonard J. Hughes and demolished in 1934 and replaced by a Tudor ballroom and shop, but the ballroom later became Marks & Spencer's, which was gutted by fire during air raids in March 1941. The branch closed in 1990.

A view of the Red Noses, 1890's. They formed part of a sandstone ridge which extended parallel with the River Mersey to Seacombe Point. Twelve years before the photo was taken, evidence was found of a Neolithic settlement. Most of the Red Noses have disappeared under the construction of the Promenade, built in the 1930's.

IVY WALLASEY

There would seem to have been no shortage of ivy growing in Wallasey of years ago. The stuff was everywhere. You see it in most of the old photographs, clinging to buildings and decorating walls and hedgerows.

The picture next page shows the ivy covered little houses which were a picturesque feature of the Liscard Village end of Urmson Road. Two little girls stand outside them in the sunlight.

It is hard to believe Liscard as a semi-rural area, but that is what it was some 110 years ago. It had shops in plenty, but it had, too, little cottages with big gardens, smithies, and fields.

There really was a mill pond in Mill Lane Old photographs show the area to have richly provided with trees – Seaview Road was a great long avenue of oaks and elms. There were quaint stiles and a sea of thatched roofs.

A curious old building was the Blue Bell Inn. The roof, covered with turf, had a luxuriant crop of grass growing all over it. The little place disappeared at the turn of the last century. The site would become the old Fire Station and today is a car park.

Trafford House stood where the Post Office is today. It was demolished just before World War One.

Urmson's House stood opposite the old Fire Station in Liscard Village. It dated back to 1729. It lived on until 1928.

Fields and cottages and trees – that was the Liscard our (great) grandparents knew. A place of open spaces and quiet corners. And lots of ivy.

THE WALLASEY WRECKERS

The Wallasey Wreckers. Plunderers of the shore. 'Very fiends', they called them in the far-off days when the local coastline was a desolate waste of windswept sandhills. Many a ship lured to its doom. Many a half-drowned sailor sent reeling as he tottered from the water. Thefts that did not stop at violence. Violence that was no stranger to murder. Wild nights. Greed that went beserk.

Shouts of confusion. Dark deeds and the roar of the sea. A real touch of 'Jamaica Inn'.

This part of the coast had a sinister reputation. There was a report prepared by a Royal Commission in 1839.

The report stated that "on the Cheshire coast not far from Liverpool they will rob those who have escaped the perils of the sea and come safe on shore, and will mutilate dead bodies for the sake of rings or personal ornaments."

One historian, writing of the area as it was two centuries ago, described the locals as "deeply saturated with the sin of covetousness."

He went on: "On stormy days and nights crowds might be seen hurrying to the shore with carts, barrows, horses, asses, or oxen even, which were made to draw timber, bales, boxes, or anything that the raging waters might have cast up...

"Many a half-drowned sailor has had a knock on the sconce, whilst trying to obtain a footing that has sent him reeling back into the seething water..."

There is a story that one local parson was so addicted to wrecking as any of his congregation. He often led the stampede to the shore.

He would cry from his pulpit when news of a wreck was brought during service time: "Now, friends, wait till I get down from my pulpit and doff my gown, and then we all start fair."

It was not uncommon for fires to be lit along the coastline to lure some unsuspecting ship on to the treacherous Burbo or Hoyle banks, there to break up in heavy seas.

Wirral was known as a desperate region, and the Wallasey corner of it had a particularly bad name.

A seaman washed ashore received scant mercy. There was many a murder.

"Many a house has been suddenly replenished with eatables and drinkables and furniture where previously bare walls and wretched accommodation only were visible," wrote one chronicler of the late years of the 1700s.

There was a famous wreck in October, 1820. The schooner *Mary Betsy*, from Wexford, drifted ashore at Leasowe.

The captain and four of the crew who were drowned were buried in Wallasey churchyard.

"No humanity was shown by anyone on that shore," said a report at the time.

Local wreckers completely stripped the vessel. It was said they left nothing but the standing rigging and the masts.

A grave or pit discovered during the building of New Brighton Palace, over 130 years ago, revealed evidence that it had been used for the purpose of concealing wreckers' spoils.

It was said that human remains were found. Skeletons of sailors done to death by plunderers on the sands.

In spite of the activity of the local coastguards in later years, many of the residents of Wallasey, if a wreck occurred in the night from which merchandise was washed ashore, were ready to assert "seeking's finding and finding's keepers".

Local fishermen were reputed to use their nets and their boats as a "blind" for highly illegal activities.

A certain sandhill was many years ago found to be covered with sugar. A hogshead of sugar washed ashore had been rolled to the point and then broken up.

The "sugar hill" was popular with children. They put the mixture of sugar and sand in their mouths, sucked the sugar, and spat out the sand.

The scene that followed the wreck of the brig *Elizabeth Buckham*, on 26th November, 1866, was described in the Wallasey News in the 1930's by historian Bertram Furniss:

"She went ashore and broke up before assistance could be rendered. Laden with rum and coconuts which floated ashore ...

"On the shore casks of rum were breached; some carried the spirit to their houses, others drank it on the spot ...

"Fights ensured, and the whole police force of Wallasey (five in number) was quite inadequate to cope with the tumult...

"Towards evening they were fully occupied lifting the sleeping carousers to a safe place above high water mark to prevent their being drowned by the rising tide..."

At least two deaths occurred. There were comments at the inquests. It took Wallasey a long time to live it down.

All of that was ugly enough, but it was nothing compared with the goings-on of earlier days. The late 1700's were the dark period of wrecking and smuggling.

They were days when Old Mother Redcap's Cottage, check by jowl with the sandhills, was the gathering place for those who took what they shouldn't by fair means or foul.

Early in the 18th Century Mother Redcap's became a tavern. It was noted for its strong home-brewed ale. It became a haunt of the wreckers of the Wirral coastline. Smugglers used it. It was a clearing house for contraband.

Over the years it went under various names. The Red House, the Halfway House, and Seabank Cottage.

When Mother Redcap lived is not quite certain. Probably in the late 18th and early 19th century. She was said to be a handsome woman who always wore a red cap or hood. She was assisted in her tavern by a pretty niece. Mother Redcap was the friend of all seafarers. They trusted her completely. She looked after their prize money and pay. She protected them from the attention of the press gang.

Intruders forcing open the front door were shot into the cellar by an automatic trap-door. They were presumably then suitably dealt with by Mother Redcap and her associates.

Contraband was hidden in the ceilings over oak beams, which stood on either side of the fireplace in both ground floor and rooms. Smugglers and sailors hid their money in wall cavities. In one room was a hiding place, large enough to contain a man, contrived in the thickness of the wall and with an entrance from the floor above.

Near the south end of the house was a large underground chamber roofed with paving stones and supported by beams. Leading out of it was a secret passage giving access to a deep ditch half way up what is now Lincoln Drive. The ditch ended in a deep hollow fringed with rushes ad sheltered by a large willow tree used for smugglers as a look-out. In the hollow pack-horses were loaded with contraband. The destination of much of it was Chester. Acting as banker for many of those coming under her roof, Mother Redcap is reputed to have acquired considerable wealth.

Under the main stairway of the house itself was an exit from the cellar leading into the yard. In the yard was a dry well over twelve feet deep, at the bottom of which was an entrance into the underground chamber. Across the yard and beyond the well was a malt-house where they brewed the tavern's famous ale. The beverage was dark brown in colour and lace with Jamaican rum.

Close in front of the house was an anchorage known as Red Brett's Pool. This was used by privateer vessels and preventive coastguard sloops. The pool was formed by a stream which flowed to the west of the house. This supplied fresh water to the ships and Mother Redcap's brewery. In front of the house was a dummy weather vane. It was rotated in accordance with pre-arranged signals.

The house was bought in the 1880's by Joseph Kitchingman. It was then being used as a fisherman's cottage. During considerable alterations made by Kitchingman a small cannon was unearthed in the grounds. It was a bow-chaser as used on privateers in the 1790's. Kitchingman found a small stone with nine holes cut into its square surface. Coins were thrown at the holes in a game called 'pitch penny'. The stone was supposed to have been made by French prisoners of war in Napoleonic times, when they were on parole from prisons in Liverpool.

There is a story that in 1690, when the troops of William III were encamped near Leasowe awaiting embarkation for Ireland, despatches were conveyed via Mother Redcap's to boats in the Mersey.

The cottage, demolished in 1974, was said to be the hiding place of many barrels and bales. Its thick walls held many secrets.

Ponies trotted across to Bidston marshes in the night, laden with spoils from the shore. There were tricks galore to fool the forces of law and order.

Romantic and colourful? Only, I think, in adventure tales and period novels.

They were the days when for the sake of a ring on his finger or a ribbon of lace around his neck a sailor would be coldly murdered as he struggled ashore from a wreck.

Years of cruelty and greed. Years of violence.

There was little kindness or mercy in them. Fights and killings and grab.
Years when those who sailed the seas feared to be thrown adrift along the local coast.
Years when this was a local prayer

God bless father and
God bless mother, and
God send us a wreck afore morning.

OLD COURT YARD

The picture overleaf is that of Albert Terrace which stood off Mount Pleasant Road. It was one of the many little courts and alleys of old Wallasey. It disappeared a long time ago. In the picture can be seen the communal pump which stood at the centre of the terrace. A girl sits beside it and another peeps out from a doorway of a house on the right.

The Wallasey of these little girls was slow-moving and gaslit. It had a long way to go before the march of time was to catch up with it and change it completely.

Places like this may not have boasted any mod cons, but it had a real identity. It was not exactly picturesque, but it had a certain charm. What they had, and in generous measure, was warmth, vitality and friendliness. They were close communities, Their people cared about one another.

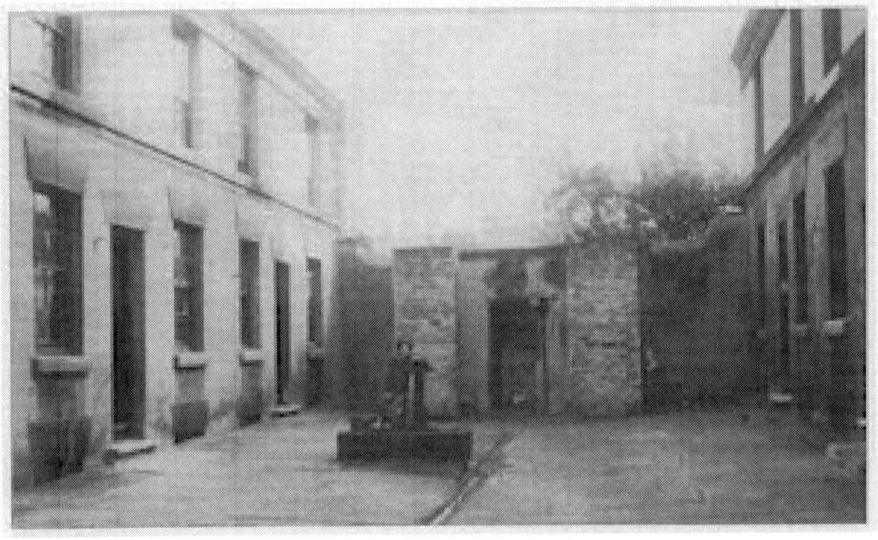

NAMING YOUR STREET

Many of the names that were given to the streets had a story behind them. The names were tied up with the history. They help to build up a picture of the past. Unfortunately many streets have disappeared under the bulldozers and tower blocks or flats as well as vast estates now occupy the sites.

Seacombe got its main street in the middle of the 19th Century. It was called Victoria Road to honour Queen Victoria. Today of course it is known as Borough Road.

Around Borough Road many new terraces of small houses sprang up. Some of the roads got their names from local historical or geographical connections.

Poulton Road was the road leading to the leafy village of the name, close by Wallasey Pool.

Bellevue Road, which was half-up rooted to make way for the

second Mersey tunnel, marked the site of Bellevue Gardens which once lay between St. Paul's Church and old Victoria Road. Demesne Street derives its name from having been cut through land belonging to Rear-Admiral Smith, Lord of the Manor of Poulton.

Some famous names are commemorated by roads nearby such as Beaconsfield Road after Lord Beaconsfield, Beatrice Street after Princess Beatrice, Leopold Street after Prince Leopold and Gladstone Road after the Prime Minister, William E. Gladstone. Other interesting road names in the Seacombe area are those who are connected with prominent local residents. Byerley Street was called after Dr. Isaac Byerley, who lived in Myrtle Cottage. He was a popular doctor in the middle of the 19th Century.

Nelson Street, one time off Brighton Street, owes its name to Philip Nelson, a Liverpool ship-owner. Ellis Street was called after John Ellis, who built the unique Concertina Cottages, off Wheatland Lane.

Littledale Road commemorates Harold Littledale who lived in the manor house that was the College of Art in Central Park.

Rappart Road honoured D.B. Rappart, who played a great part in the development of Wallasey between 1884 and 1914.

The Mainwaring family owned the land in Seacombe and their name was given to Mainwaring Road.

Another road of the past was Vienna Street. So called because Emmanuel Kopetzki, who came from Vienna, Austria, built the Vienna Hall (later to become the Marina Cinema), in Brighton Street.

In the early years of the 20th Century builders in the area of Wheatland Lane, where once it was wheat fields, showed a partiality for naming roads after lakes and poets – Geneva and Lucerne, Byron, Milton and Shakespeare. Some of these streets barely exist in name.

In Poulton, Gorsedale Road was originally called Cinder Lane. In those far off days it was a beautiful walk, bordered by yellow gorse bushes and trees. Gorsey Lane took its name from them.

Running up from the Dock Road near Gorsey Lane was Creek Side, whose name recalls the time Wallasey Pool was not confined between dock walls.

The district of Somerville may have obtained its name from a house built by James Fisher. His house shows on old maps as Somerville House. Moving along Poulton Road is Sherlock Lane which perpetuates the name of a family resident in Wallasey since early times. Captain Sherlock was the last captain of the ferry sailing boats between Liverpool and Seacombe.

Mill Lane takes its name from the fine old mill which once stood by Eric Road.

St. Hilary Brow was originally called Carren Hill after a family of that name.

In 1901 Harrison Drive was opened, and called after the local family who gave Harrison Park to the town. Claremount Road was once called Top Lane. It appears to have taken its name from the Rev. William Green's private school, which he called Clare College, his old college at Cambridge.

Hose Side Road is a modern adaption of the word 'Hoose', itself a corruption of Hoes' – sandhills. In its earlier days this was a lane which lay alongside sandhills. Broadway Avenue was once called Townfield Lane, and a footpath ran from the road across the fields to Seaview Road – from which the sea really could be viewed. This footpath, which took the route of Kirkway, was nicknamed Suicide Lane., A man staying at the old Hotel Victoria, New Brighton, shot his two children and then himself on the spot.

Seaview Road had originally been Marsden's Lane, after Mr. Marsden, who built a highly ornate house called Liscard Castle – after we get Castle and Turrets Roads. The names of two more roads in the area were derived from houses situated near their sites – Oarside Drive and The Laund.

Kirkway takes its name from a legendary Saxon church supposedly situated near to the road.

Vyner Road was named after the Vyner family, big local landowners. Meddowcroft takes its name from another landowner.

Love Lane in Liscard was at one time a charming walk, popular with courting couples. In the old days it was referred to as Cuff Lane, for it bordered a field called Cuff Hey. Monk Road and Newell Road were named in honour of Thomas Monk and his son-in-law and partner, constructors of the Great Float Docks and Seacombe Ferry approaches.

The name Rake Lane is particularly curious. The word rake means lane, and so the road is virtually Lane Lane.

In Egremont is King Street after Ellen King, who owned the land. Tobin Street is named after Sir John Tobin, the local squire. Withens Lane was probably given its name because it led into a filed called The Withens. Townfield Lane, now Urmson Road (named after Urmson House which stood in Liscard Village until 1928), was in the old days the way to Liscard Village, part of it between Rake Lane and Withens Lane.

Trafalgar Road was formerly Abbott's Lane, after an old local resident. Stringhey Road perpetuates another field name. Zig Zag Road obtained its name from its tortuous course. Magazine Brow is part of old Wallasey, and close by it lay the old gunpowder store. Other local residents commemorated by roads in the district are Mrs Maddock (Lady of the Manor), John Penkett, (Lord of the Manor), Richard Steel and Joseph Walmsley (members of the old Urban District Council). Atherton Street was named after the man who developed the north end of New Brighton, James Atherton, He was a retired Liverpool merchant who came to New Brighton in 1832. Rowson Street is called after Atherton's son-in-law, who is buried in St. Hilary's churchyard. Local benefactor Frederick North gave his name to North Drive and the Rev. Richard Drake Fowell, first vicar of St. James's Church, is commemorated by Fowell Road. Molyneux Drive was named after the Moyneux family, who lived on the big estate which later became the Tower Grounds.

A VIEW FROM THE TOWER

View of Magazine Brow at the junction of Mariners Road, c1912

View of Kirkway from Earlston Road, 1927

Trafalgar Road with Stringhey Road left, 1950

Other roads in the district which took their names from houses, now demolished, which stood nearby are Dalmorton and Sudworth.

In Moreton there is Fender Lane (after one of the two streams which drain the nearby marsh) and Barnston Lane, formerly called Chapel Lane after the small place of worship which stood in it. Lingham Lane was originally Lighthouse Lane, Griffin Avenue is after Canon Griffin, formerly Church of the Sacred Heart and a one time member of the Town Council.

Glasier Road, Snowdon Road and Hardie Avenue are all named after politicians. Burden Road and Eleanor Road recall two of the early pioneers of Moreton, Charlie Burden and his wife Eleanor. Both served on the Town Council. Both fought for the area in the 1920's, when it was unkindly christened 'Bungalow Town'.

Wallasey has seen many roads disappear in the 1960's. The Town Council has chosen names for the new estates. Mainly names of birds, flowers and trees. Not very imaginative. The old names marked a time in history. The old landmarks are gone and so has the local history with each phase of development.

WALLASEY IN THE 1940'S

The first half of the 1940's were years of war, of bombs and blackout, of queues and coupons. The next five were of peace, of permits and town planning. It was the decade of sirens, and then a fresh start.

The first year of the 1940's was strangely quiet. Thousands of children had been evacuated. The sirens didn't sound until June, 1940, and then it was a false alarm.

After eleven months of the 'phoney' war, Wallasey had its first air raid on August 10, 1940, It was just a taste of what was to come.

Over 500 alerts followed between then and January, 1942. In addition to 340 townspeople killed, 275 were seriously injured. Over 1,150 houses were demolished. Over 17,000 were damaged. Wallasey was a front-line town.

King George VI and Queen Elizabeth came on 6th November, 1940. It was intended to be a hush-hush visit, but the news got round and the crowds turned out.

Inspecting bombed streets during their tour, the King and Queen chatted to many families who had lost their homes only a few nights before. Rubble was everywhere.

It was a visit full of little human incidents – like the Queen waving to two old ladies she spotted sitting on their doorsteps a good distance away, and the King's comment, "Don't tread on my corns!" to a section of the crowd which almost completely surrounded him at one point.

"And where do you live, dear?" asked the Queen of one little girl in Seacombe, "Back of the Gandy" was the enlightening reply.

Prime Minister Winston Churchill came on April 25, 1941. Complete with cigar and V-sign, he inspected Civil Defence services.

"Good old Winston" shouted the crowd which seemed to have appeared from nowhere. Before leaving for the Merseyside docks, he turned to the people who had greeted him and called "God bless you all".

The following Sunday evening, in one of his memorable broadcasts, he made reference to his country-wide tour the previous week. It had the effect, he said, of bracing his own courage; it had stimulated his own spirit.

Wallasey liked to think that some part of that process derived from his brief visit here.

In 1942, in the middle of a hot summer, Wallasey Home Guard defended the town against mock invaders. It was a realistic bit of work. It showed just what could happen.

Then the G.I's came. Hundreds of American troops were accommodated at New Brighton. The New Palace Cafeteria became their canteen. They lived at the Tower Ballroom. They were favourites with the girls. They were generous guests. Chewing gum and chocolate was regularly handed out to local youngsters who had to manage on a weekly sweets ration of something like four ounces.

Serious bomb damage on Church Street, junction of Church Avenue, looking towards King Street, 20 March 1941

Wallasey gave the Americans freedom of the town in 1944. They paraded through the streets, and in a Vale Park ceremony the "Old Glory" fluttered alongside the Union Jack.

The war brought boom business to the cinemas. There were long queues outside them all in Wallasey.

Folk went to see "Mrs. Miniver". "The Foreman Went To France", "The Way Ahead", "Went The Day Well", and "The First of the Few".

Other films included "The Wicked Lady", "The Man in Grey", "49th Parallel, "In Which We Serve", "Millions Like Us", and the Bing Crosby-Bob Hope "Road" films.

Wallasey people brought gramophone records of the Andrews Sisters, the Ink Spots, Vera Lynn (the 'Forces' Sweetheart), Kenny Baker, and George Formby.

Everyone was humming tunes like 'Begin The Beguine', 'Room Five-hundred and Four', 'White Cliffs of Dover', 'Somewhere Over The Rainbow'.

There was Charlie Kunz at the piano, Adelaide Hall, Tessie O'Shea, the Western Brothers, Stainless Stephen, Gillie Potter, Suzette Tarry, Elsie and Doris Waters.

On the radio people listened to shows like 'Garrison Theatre'. Bebe Daniels and Ben Lyon in 'Hi Gang!' and ITMA, with Tommy Handley.

There was the Nine O'Clock News, with Big Ben from London before it. There was Lord Haw-Haw from Germany. He mentioned Wallasey by name on two occasions.

The ferryboats were blacked out. One of them, the 'Royal Daffodil II', was sunk at her berth in a raid in May, 1941. It was a direct hit, but despite the violence of the explosion, only one man suffered. He was blown out of the engine-room and lost his false teeth! It was thirteen months before the vessel was salvaged. She looked a sad and battered sight – no funnel, no mast, smothered in marine growth, and full of tons of sand.

The 'Queen of the Fleet', they had called her once. She had lost her elegance, but she was repaired and put back into service in June, 1943.

Small Rations

Thousands of sandbags were used throughout the town as protection against blast and bomb splinters. Communal shelters hugged the pavements in score of streets.

Rations were small. A few ounces of this, a half-pound of that. A thing like an orange was practically nothing but a memory from pre-war days.

British restaurants provided cheap meals to the public. There was one in St. Paul's Road, Seacombe, another in Wallasey Road. 'Clippies' collected the fares on the buses. They wore slacks and head scarves.

There were queues outside all the shops. There was a Food Control office in Liscard.

The Home Guard had its headquarters in the School of Art, Central Park. There were barrage balloons.

Short of Beer

There was a shortage of beer in the pubs. Some hostelries introduced their own rationing system.
There was coupons for utility clothes. The girls, troubled by a shortage of stockings, painted their legs.
Wallasey had 'Wings For Victory' weeks. There was also 'Salute the Soldiers' weeks.
Cigarettes were as hard to come by as gold. There were 'under the counter' dealings.
Wallasey folk were urged by posters to remember that careless talk cost lives. People were asked to save every bit of scrap. Dustbins were provided for unwanted peelings. They went to feed pigs and poultry.
George Reakes, an Independent, had succeeded Lieut-Colonel Moore-Brbazon as Wallasey's wartime M.P. Conservative Ernest Marples defeated him in 1945.
There were bonfires and parades when the war ended in 1945. There were 'victory cruises' on the ferryboats.
A shy young V.C., Lieutenant Ian Fraser, R.N., was given a sword of honour by the town in which he had decided to make his home. Fraser had taken a midget submarine into Singapore Harbour on 31st July 1945 to attack the crack Japanese cruiser '*Takao*' with limpet bombs.

Street Parties

During the victory celebrations people chalked huge V-signs on every available piece of wall space. They hung up flags and buntings.
Ferryboats were dressed overall. Up on the Breck they burnt a vast mound of torn-out air raid shelter fittings.
Pianos were brought out on the pavements and there was dancing in the open. The magistrates were busy with requests for licensing extensions.

The weekly food ration was only four ounces of bacon, eight ounces of sugar, and two ounces each of butter, cheese, cooking fats and tea, but somehow everyone managed to stage a celebration.

In the new big new film that was going the local rounds, a youthful Deanna Durbin summed up the feeling of everyone: "Can't Help Singing".

Estates Born

Wallasey was quick to make a fresh start. There was bustle and plans.

In 1946, despite permits and shortages of everything, the town began to re-build, replace and improve.

The shelters came tumbling down. Houses started going up.

The first of the vast new estates were taking shape at Leasowe and Moreton within months of the end of hostilities. New schools went on the drawing boards.

The last of the luggage boats sailed from Seacombe in March, 1947. The Rakers were re-formed and went to a home at the Tower.

In the late 1940's Wallasey spread itself out and stretched itself up. Its shape changed completely, It got itself a new look.

The decade that had opened to the noise of sirens and bombblasts closed to be cheerful, heartening music of bulldozers clearing blitz sites, and the rattle of bricklayers' trowels.

A VIEW FROM THE TOWER

FLORAL PAVILION THEATRE
NEW BRIGHTON   Phone: 051-639 4360   Licensee: F. G. Leyland

Week Commencing Monday, September 15th, 1980
Evenings at 7.15 p.m.   Saturday at 6.30 p.m. and 8.45 p.m.

DEPARTMENT OF LEISURE SERVICES presents
MR. DON ELLIS
FOR THE 24th CONSECUTIVE YEAR
1956 - 1980
WITH HIS

OLDE TYME MUSIC HALL

starring

PERCY **EDWARDS** THE BIRD MAN	JACK **STOREY** BLACKPOOL COMEDIAN
KITTY **GILLOW** MALE IMPERSONATOR	TOMMY **JAMES** THE CONCERTINA KING

MISS ELSIE SMITH'S CAN CAN GIRLS

GRAHAM JARVIS A SMILE AND A SONG	**NORMAN SCOTT** MUSICAL DIRECTOR

DON ELLIS
YOUR HOST CHAIRMAN AND FRIEND

PRICES: £1.40 & £1.00   Pensioners & Children £1.00 & 60p
CAR PARK   -   CAFE   -   BARS

G. & M. Organ Ltd., Theatrical Printers, Wrington, Bristol.

WALLASEY'S WORLD FAMOUS FARM

Model Farm stood along Mill Lane, in Liscard. It was the "pet" of merchant Harold Littledale, a local squire. Littledale was the son-in-law of Sir John Tobin, who lived at Liscard Hall (later the School of Art and now demolished). The house was built in the 1820's. Sir John was the builder of St. John's Church. Liscard Road. His son, the Rev. John Tobin, was its first vicar.

Sir John died in 1851 and was buried in the churchyard of St. John's Church. Littledale succeeded him at the Hall. By 1845 he had established the 440 acres of arable farm land. It was a show piece with Mr. Torr, of Lincoln, the best practical farmer of the time, who directed its lay-out.

It was described as "unquestionably one of the greatest lions of the day, which is proved by its being almost daily visited by everyone who takes an interest in agriculture."

The entrance into the farm was in what is now Rullerton Road. The farmhouse still stands at the corner of Eldon Road, engulfed by urban development.

The Liscard in which it stood had picturesque cottages, whitewashed and thatched-roofed. There were stiles and horse troughs. In Martins Lane there was a dark well. The records give its depth as being over 160 feet.

As far as possible, everything about Model Farm was designed to co-operate smooth working and the elimination of waste, Efficiency was its motto.

Its water supply came from its own pond. This had an island in the centre with grass and trees. There was a special house for the bailiff. There was a dairy, with a staff of trim dairy maids. Piggeries were fitted with patent troughs. There were rick-yards, places for curing bacon, a slaughter house, and a super smithy.

Steam power was introduced – very advanced for that period. An engine thrashed and ground corn, cut the cattle foods, and churned milk.

Littledale spared no expense. The farm was his passion. He was tremendously proud of it. He loved showing it off, and had plenty of opportunity. As news of it spread, agricultural students came from all parts of Europe to see it. There were learned papers on it. It became known as something very special. It was big. It was ambitious. It was as neat and orderly as a barrack square.

The farm enclosure had boundary lines of trees. It formed a self-contained centre of well-ordered industry.

Littledale pioneered new ways. He was among the first to apply science to farming.

Cottages were built for the workers. They stood along Mill Lane and Rullerton Road. There were shippons and stables. Great hay-yards. Pedigree cattle.

The sheep farm section was on the Wallasey Golf links. The shepherd's house stood at the end of Green Lane.

Shippons and stables were drained into a huge tank, which led by underground pipes to the various fields.

Farm fields in the area of Martins Lane and Liscard Road were noted for "wonderful grass and corn crops."

Corn was also produced between what are now Central Park Avenue and Serpentine Road. Belvidere Road was originally only an accommodation road for the farm.

Littledale's enterprise became the envy of other farms in Cheshire. He was doing big, new things.

Harold Littledale died in 1889 and the estate was purchased by the Council and some of it now forms part of Central Park.

THE BEGINNINGS OF WALLASEY FOOTBALL

Football in Wallasey was born in kick-abouts on the shore. The kick-about boys became clubs. The clubs won big followings. The football followers became fanatics. Over a century ago, before the Kop became an institution, before scarf-wrapped and rattle-waving thousands clicked through turnstiles into part of daily life, Wallasey had earned the reputation of being "a football-mad place". The game was very much the thing.
At the turn of the last century almost every church and school had its own team. There were street teams by the dozen.
Street gas lamp standards and rolled-up coats served as goalposts. Lads would pool precious pocket money to buy a ball.

Seacombe United F.C., when they were champions of the Wirral Intermediate Division in 1908-09.

Many of the teams were called after the road or area from which they came – Ashville from Ashville Road, in Seacombe, for instance, and Harrowby from Harrowby Road, close to Egremont shore, where the team trained.

The fortunes of the various clubs were followed with tremendous interest.

In days when there was no radio or television, and not much money to spare for entertainment, Saturday matches drew big crowds.

Rivalry between teams was intense. The game was taken very seriously.

Working lads – and shop and factory hours were long – were no sooner home before they were rigged out in shorts and boots and jerseys.

There were fields in plenty for games, and in Seacombe, Egremont and New Brighton the sands were clean, firm and wide. Just over 110 years ago organised games really came into their own. Football became a local craze.

Rakers, 1947-48

Although the town was growling quite rapidly and the builders were busy putting up terraces of houses, there was a great deal of open spaces available for recreation.

Football was being played at Rake Lane as long ago as 1880. All amateur stuff, of course.

New Brighton Athletic F.C

Professional football did not come to town until 1921, with the formation of the New Brighton A.F.C. (Rakers).

Over a century ago there were so many amateur teams in Wallasey that it was reported that difficulty was being found in "choosing different combinations of playing colours".

In the early years of the last century Poulton Rovers were important in the Liverpool League.

The Johnnies (Egremont St. John's) were another team to be reckoned with. "Very fast", said a contemporary report.

Poulton Rovers had Owen Jones as goalkeeper. The team started as a bible class and played on a pitch where Surrey Street is. Poulton Athletic played at Limekiln Lane.

Among the Poulton side was George Sutton, Marshall Grant and Stan Robinson – "probably the best amateur outside-left in local football".

It had Henry Upton and the Hulses and the Addisons. Names everyone knew in the old days. Harrowby had Billy Robinson, the Rudges, the Browns, Farrel, Ball and Swain, Harry Myers and Harold Fayre.

Fayre turned professional and played with Everton, Bury and Wigan Borough. He lived in Glyn Road, Wallasey, and died in 1964.

Harrowby were all-conquering. In the 1919-20 season they completed a notable triple by winning the Cheshire Amateur Cup, the Wirral Senior Cup and the West Cheshire League Shield. The teams in their great season included Hunter, Whiteford, Cleator, Freeman, Reid, Williams, Jenkins, Coffey, Aust, Sutcliffe, Hayes, Wadeson, Robertson and Cheeseborough.

There were the Seacombe, Swifts, the Riverside Lads and the Invinsa League. There were the old Wirral Senior League with such teams as Seacombe P.S.A., the old Wheatland , Liscard Kems. Rake Lane P.S.A., and Wallasey Village.

The letters P.S.A.? They stood for Pleasant Sunday Afternoon!

Seacombe Congs star in the old days was a Cyril Whitehead. He had a trial with Tranmere Rovers and later joined Northern Nomads.

Wallasey Y.M.C.A. (Manor Road) had a big name in the 1920s. In the Invinsa League it once played the Laird Street, Birkenhead, team which had a promising lad called Dixie Dean.

Memories of Moreton amateurs include the days when the local vicar was paid a yearly rent of £10 for the use of a field. In the summer the football boys rented it out to a farmer for grazing and pocketed £4 to swell their funds.

At that time a football cost 7s 6d. shirts, half-a-crown, and boots about 4s.

Wagonettes to such outlandish places as Heswall and Neston for away games cost teams a few shillings. Referees were paid a fee of 2s.

Collections were made in a cap after many games. Spectators gave what they could spare – usually coppers.

The lads played charity matches. Hospitals were then voluntary organisations and depended to a very great extent on local fund-raising activities.

If a player was injured, there would be a match organised to help him out financially.

It is recalled many years later by a spectator who watched the games that "Competition was intense, but things were kept friendly. There were very, very few ugly incidents. Football in the old days was clean and full of action. Lads would play hard for the whole game. Perhaps it was because there wasn't much else for youngsters to do in those times, but the fact is that Wallasey probably had more small clubs than any town in the area".

The changes over the years have been in amateur football what they have been in everything else – tremendous.

Teams don't dress behind hedges anymore, or shield one another if there are no hedges conveniently to hand.

You see few lads pedal-cycling or running to a match. They arrive in cars at laid-out pitches.

Sport was something to battle your heart out for, something to run the legs from under you for.

It hadn't become too organised. It hadn't become something of a business.

It was practice on the wide clean sands.

It was a cup you carried home to the sideboard, to keep polished and cherished right through the years into memory-filled old age.

WHEN POULTON WAS FAMOUS FOR ITS TREES

Its trees made old Poulton a place its people were proud of. Great oaks and fine elms. Rich and heavily-scented lilac trees in the gardens of fine houses. Avenues of ash and poplar where buildings and roads now stand. The woods were old when Poulton was a small village. They seemed somehow to guard it from the developers of the early 1900s, held at bay for a time the progress that the 1920s brought to the rest of the town. Poulton kept its old-world look rather longer than its neighbouring villages of Seacombe and Liscard.
'Poulton' was there at the time of 'Domesday', and probably before. Arable and grassland lay about it.

From along Limekiln Lane to Birkenhead there was in old times a ferry service, crossing approximately where Duke Street Bridge now stands.

View of the Penny Bridge and Toll, c1900

Passengers were carried in what was known as the "'Poulton cock boat', an old name for a yawl; two masted fore-and-aft rigged sailing boat.

Many, many years later the Halfpenny Bridge was built. The 1843 bridge was constructed of wood. In 1896 the toll to cross it was increased to one penny.

The name 'Penny Bridge' has stuck, despite the fact that the old bridge was replaced, first by a swing bridge, and later to a static bridge and the crossing made toll-free.

Men looking for work on the Birkenhead side who did not have sufficient money for the tolls would pass their clothes to friends who passed over the bridge whilst they swam the short distance.

Close by the bridge was the 'Old House', or Bird's House, built in 1697, at the corner of Limekiln Lane and Poulton Bridge Road. It still stands today, probably the oldest complete house in Wallasey.

Poulton Road, Autumn 1914

The old Pool Inn faced down Poulton Bridge Road, standing a little south of the previous demolished one. The first one was demolished over 130 years ago. The latter just a few years ago.

Gone are the memories of the open meadows and the waving cornfields through which a path ran between Liscard and Somerville.

Gone also is Poulton Hall, a large four-square building which stood on the site of the present Poulton Hall Road, until 1933.

Another stately brick house, of late 18th century design, was Poulton Manor House, entered from Sherlock Lane. It was demolished about 1905.

How the district of Somerville obtained its name is not clear, but it seems likely that it may have been derived from a house built by a Mr. James Fisher and shown on maps of the area over one hundred and fifty years ago as "Somerville".

Sherlock Lane perpetuates the name of a family resident in Wallasey since early times. Captain Sherlock was the last skipper of

the ferry sailing boats between Seacombe and Liverpool.
The Jolly Sailor was a Poulton pub of the past. Little more than a country cottage, it stood in Limekiln Lane.
It was serving ale up to the early 1920's.
Near Gorsey Lane was Robinson Creek, a stretch of water which in 1896 was the scene of a skating accident in which several boys lost their lives.
And there was Darley Dene. Originally as The Slopes. It was built and lived in for many years by Mr. Monk.
In World War Two Darley Dene was used as a military quarters. In an air raid on 12th March, 1941, it received a direct hit, killing some soldiers and injuring many others.
Just up on Breck Road was Heathbank, occupied by a Mr. McInnes, a well-known philanthropic character in the district. The house and grounds were later used as a social club for mill workers.
A hundred years ago Poulton still had its village water pump and trough. They were right in the centre of the cross roads of Poulton Road, Mill Lane, Breck Road and Poulton Bridge Road.
An old Cheshire rhyme praised 'Poulton for trees', and with good cause. It was a part of town rich in them.
They stretched in long avenues. Between Somerville and where the Pool Inn once stood, there were hundreds.
There was a stream from Mill Lane to the Pool. There was fishing in it at one time.
Poulton had its mill, the Rake Mill, and there was a field known as Mill Hey. One of the houses later built on the field was called Mill Bank. It then became Clarendon High School and today is a funeral home.
The Eyrie, on Breck Road, was one of the first large houses built in the area. It was there up to the 1930's. It was for many years the home of Mr. William Carson, ferry manager, who designed and constructed the Egremont Ferry of 1874, the New Brighton Ferry of 1865. And the Seacombe Ferry of 1880.
There were little shops on corners, with clanging doorbells, and everything weighed and wrapped by hand. Along Poulton Road,

towards where the Pool Inn once stood, were Ivy, Madeira, Alma and Rose cottages. Somerville Boys' School was remembered by its old headmaster, Mr. A.W. Heap. Somerville Girls School had Miss Delaney as headmistress.

Jolly Sailor Inn, Limekiln Lane

St. Luke's Church was built in 1900 (previously services were held in a temporary iron building in Limekiln Lane). Its roof and steeple were destroyed in the air raids of 1941.

A street directory of a hundred years ago listed 'garden allotments' between York Road and Brentwood Street.

Poulton got its first picture house when the Queen's Picture House opened on 4th November 1911. The cinema closed in 1959 and became a petrol filling station and then a supermarket. The cinema was small and intimate – it never tried the neon signs of its chromium-and-plush big brothers – the Queen's was a cinema that made many friends. So did its manager, Dick Rutherford. Its gas lights spluttered. Mr. Rutherford was at its doors at the end of the evening performance to say goodnight to everyone.

The old Queen's was small and friendly. It had atmosphere. It

had character.
Just like the place it served. Just like Poulton as it used to be.

THE SCHOOL BORN ON A FERRYBOAT

Wallasey High School – first school of its kind in the town – was born on a small ferryboat crossing the Mersey on a sunny day one-hundred and fifty years ago. Walking the deck of the good ship '*Crocus*', the vicars of Seacombe and Poulton saw many girls of high school age travelling to Liverpool for their education. They thought it unfair that while the boys of the town had the Grammar School the girls had nothing at all. The clergymen decided to gather interested persons and start a school on high school lines. In 1883 the 'High' started life.

Two rooms on the ground floor of the Liscard Concert Hall were secured and 30 or 40 pupils, with screens dividing the rooms into four compartments, began to learn the refined accomplishments of the 1880s.

Later the school moved to Manor Road (Stringhey Road corner), where the girls occupied two houses.

Drill was taught by a sharp-mannered sergeant. Department was regarded as being very important.

Memories once recorded by a pupil during the school's first years refer to draughty horse-trams, slow and uncertain. Bicycles for girls were unheard of.

Manor Road Concert Hall, 1880s

Walking was no hardship on fine bright mornings, but in bad weather the going was not so easy.

The girls trudged through sand which drifted across the roads. Whatever happened, they had to arrive by nine o'clock.

School mornings in those days began with a hymn, a prayer and bible reading, and then on to drill.

At 11 o'clock there was 10-minute break for lunch. The girls had preparation and special subjects in the afternoon. There was a weekly sewing class.

Visiting mistresses instructed in drawing, dancing, and German. There were botany rambles in the wide fields in Liscard.

They found wild flowers along the hedges in Seaview Road, then shaded with trees. Large iron gates closed the road from Hoseside to the Captain's Pit. An old turreted house, Liscard Castle, stood close by.

Miss Eaton was the High School's first headmistress. She had the reputation of being a strict disciplinarian.

Reports by Oxford examiners in 1896 and 1898 commended the girls for their "ladylike refined deportment" and referred to the "air of quiet refinement which pervades the whole school".

One of the reports stated: "It is evident that the object of the headmistress and her staff is not merely to give a good sound instruction to the girls but also to train them into cultured English gentle-women."

When the school roll reached the number of 100 pupils the event was celebrated by a big picnic on the sandhills of Harrison Drive.

WALLASEY AT THE PICTURES

Films came to Wallasey for the first time in September, 1907. At the Palace Theatre, New Brighton, just above the 'Ham and Egg' Parade, the Animated Picture Company put on its first programme. On 2nd October the Wallasey News reported: "An excellent evening's entertainment is provided this week at the Palace Theatre, Virginia Road. Audiences have seen animated pictures brought to the district for the first time. The films are in splendid condition. There is no eye-straining. The pictures include all the most famous of the day, depicting subjects historical, geographical and sensational. A picture showing H.M King Edward VII and all the Royal Family on board the battleship 'Dreadnought' appeals to the patriotic."

Among the early films shown at the old Palace over a century ago were 'The Mill Girl' ('a touching story of factory life'), 'The

Fisher Girl's Wooing', and 'Satan at Play' ('a real screamer'). Another film shown was 'Ali Baba and the Forty Thieves' was billed as "without doubt the most wonderful picture ever taken by hand. Cost over £10,000 to produce.

The programmes shown at first were a mixture of 'animated pictures' and live variety turns. At the opening performance at the Palace the star turn was Basco, 'the tramp cyclist'.

Prices of admission ranged from twopence to one shilling. The shows were "moral and refined, pleasing to ladies, gentlemen and children."

Other picture houses started to open after the Palace started. The Vienna Hall, Brighton Street and Tower Theatre got in on the act. They featured the Royal American Bioscope – and films like 'The Curfew Shall Not Ring Tonight'.

The cinemas became quite popular by the time of the First World War. There were half-a-dozen halls doing brisk business. The posters outside advertised the latest silent 'flickies'. Children were admitted half price and ladies were requested to remove their hats during the performances.

By 1916 there were a dozen theatres showing the latest films. One of the new picture houses was a former drill hall in King Street, Egremont which became the Royal. Later it became a snooker hall. There was also the Court, at New Brighton; the Liscard Palace; the Marina; the Kinema Picture House, Liscard Road (later the Continental); the Cosy Cosmo, Wallasey Village; the Queen's, in Poulton, and the Lyceum, at Egremont.

The Lyceum, later the Gaumont/Apollo 6, was formerly a Presbyterian church, was to go up in flames in December, 1931. The Gaumont rose from the ashes two years later.

A feature of the smaller halls was a lady would play at a piano which supplied the music suitable to the action of the film.

Local cinemas did well during the Great War. Patriotic films, full of heroics and flag waving, and jokes at the expense of the Kaiser, packed the cinemas in every night.

Gaumont, 1933

The cinemas had a boom period through the 1920's. By the mid-twenties the town had the Trocadero, the Marina, the Liscard Palace, the Palace, New Brighton, the Court, the King's, the Queen's, the Lyceum, the Royal, the Cosy Cosmo, and the Capitol.

The Capitol, later the ABC then a Mecca Bingo, was opened in August, 1926. It was called "the finest picture palace in the North". It was built on a site that had originally housed Gibbons' cab yard. Locals called it 'Alladin's Palace'. It had seating for 1,400. In 1927 the pictures found a voice. The first picture made in which words were spoken was 'The Jazz Singer'. The talkies had arrived. In the 1930's the Gaumont, big and plushy, was a luxurious addition to the cinemas of the town. Its first night was made a civic occasion. The cinema had thick carpets, bright lights and inviting neon signs.

During the blitzes the cinemas remained open and became the number one form of escape from the wartime blackouts and worries. The cinemas were packed. It was during the war that Sunday opening of the cinemas was allowed for the first time in the town.

Staff stand outside the Royal, King Street, 1963

The good times continued for the cinemas in the 1950's but increase in television ownership had a serious knock on effect and the slump began with attendance figures. Cinemas began to close. Between 1956 and 1960 six cinemas closed down. The little box in the corner of the living room began to take favour over a seat in the circle.

The slump continued through the 1970's and 1980's and more cinemas began to close. Some changed to bingo halls. Many were demolished. It was such a long time ago when you paid just a few coppers to watch comedy greats, such as Keaton, Pickford or Chaplin, and then come out of the cinema into a gas-lit street and catch the last tram home.

THE DEVIL'S NEST

'The Devil's Nest' was a cluster of little shanties and cafes which stood above the New Brighton sands nearly two centuries ago. This is one of the few paintings of it still in existence. They sprang up in the 1830's and were inhabited by a colony of donkey drivers and shore hawkers. The Nest was rather noisy and a rough community. They were cleared about 1871 and replaced by the 'Ham and Eggs Parade', which we take a look at in the next chapter.

THE HAM AND EGG PARADE

The last years of the 19th Century and the first years of the last century were years of quiet shame at up-and-coming New Brighton. The place had a skeleton, and it wasn't in a cupboard. Big, brash and vulgar, the 'Ham and Egg Parade' was there for all to see. It was a thorn in the side of Victorian and Edwardian respectability.

It earned the town a somewhat unsavoury reputation in the days of side whiskers and buttoned boots. It put it on the map long before publicity officers had been invented.

And the town squirmed with embarrassment.

The place was officially named 'Aquarium Parade' but was never called that. 'Ham and Egg' and 'Teapot Row' were the names that stuck.

The crazy narrow wooden causeway stretched a few feet above the sands from the corner of Victoria Road to a point now marked by the New Palace Arcade.
It had stalls and booths and boarding houses along its 450 yards. There were shooting galleries and fortune tellers parlours. There were wooden steps down to the rich soft sand.
It was a street hawkers' paradise. Vendors lined its ramshackle walk.
"Nice fresh shrimps a ha'penny gill". "Ripe ber-nannis, fower a penny".
And it wasn't only a hawkers' paradise. Large and prominent notices bore the advice: "Beware of Pickpockets".
The then Wallasey Urban District Council tried to pretend it did not exist. Local magistrates could not. Regular outbreaks of trouble brought many trippers before the court.
It was notable for a rowdyism unknown in other parts of the town. There were fights. There were, it was said, "goings on".

The parade was bought by the Council in May, 1907. They paid £41,500 for it.

The last of it fell beneath the workmen's hammers just over a year later. The town applauded its removal. A sore had gone.

The 'Wallasey News' reported at the time: "The associations of the 'Ham and Egg' not only checked the rise of New Brighton. They were going a long way towards its effectual ruin...

"The passing of the old parade has been regretted by none, and the announcement of its disappearance has been hailed with satisfaction and delight in most of the newspapers in the country. The development of the new scheme is being watched with interest."

The 'new scheme' included what were known as Victoria Gardens and the beginning of a decent promenade.

DAYS OF DOLE AND STRUGGLE

Much of Wallasey has been described in this book as full of pretty cottages, lovely gardens, the friendly rattling tramcars and tree-lined lanes but there was a darker side. There was real poverty at the beginning of the last century. Most of it was to be found in the little streets of Seacombe and Poulton, with a hinterland at New Brighton.

In 1905 beer was 1½d a pint, butter was 8d lb, and tobacco was between 2d and 3d an ounce. A great many did not have the money to afford the prices. A great many did not have jobs.

Each week the Seacombe Hot Pot Fund handed out meals to needy families. "At this time the cry of the poor is more than commonly compelling," said the Wallasey News in 1905.

The Board of Guardians reported that the Workhouse was full. Not everyone during the Edwardian era was happy, safe and sure. Under-nourishment was a common cause of sickness – and death. Barefoot children were a familiar sight. So were rickets and open sores.

World War One brought plenty of work. The munition factories and public services needed all the men and women they could get. It was not until the Great War that many local families knew what regular meals were. The meals may not have been large – there was rationing, bread was nearly black – but they were certain.

The 1920's opened full of bright hopes. The war to end wars was done with. The boys had come home. The shops were full. Wages weren't big – a shop girl got about 15s a week – but things were cheap.

A girl could buy a dress for 9s 6d. A pair of art silk stocking – nylons were in the future – cost her 1s 3d.

You could send your son to Wallasey Grammar School for £4 a term. New-laid eggs were a shilling a dozen. A weekly ferry contract was 1s 6d.

"Comfortable lodgings, full board" averaged 22s a week. You could buy a house in Grove Road for £720.

Jobs got scarcer in the middle years of the Twenties. Then came the General Strike. The big stoppage was born at midnight on 3rd May, 1926. Wallasey felt the effects. Trams and buses were suspended for a time. "Motor owners are expected to fill every vacant seat in their cars while travelling to and from work," said posters.

As acting secretary of the Trades' Union, Walter Citrine (later Lord), a young electrician from Wallasey, had his signature attached to all letters that passed between the T.U.C. and the Prime Minister.

Bicycles were the town's main means of transport. At Seacombe Ferry they were stacked five and six deep. Some were even piled one on top of the other.

Notices everywhere. Coal on ration. Bread in short supply. Special constables on patrol. The effects were long lasting. There followed years of depression.

In January, 1929, the 'Wallasey News' reported on "the plight of the unemployed in the town who are compelled to attend the Labour Exchange" (then in Brighton Street).

"Sometimes the queue stretches to the top of the Guinea Gap. A column of men ill-clad and insufficiently nourished."

Men went from door-to-door – pathetic carriers of battered cases containing cheap brushes, polishes, bits and pieces sold her coppers.

The early 1930's were little better for a large slice of the population. There was the Means Test Public Assistance, and grocers; and doctors' bills that could not be paid.

There was a Welfare Centre in St. Paul's Road, Seacombe. Men who were out of work undertook boot repairing, carpentry, and mat-making. It was a case of anything to keep them occupied, anything to defy Giant Despair.

In 1934 there were over 4,000 men jobless. It was a big figure for the population of the time. Things were really bad. The Wallasey News said: "Grave concern is felt here about the steadily increasing number of unemployed. It has reached a total in excess of anything before recorded in the history of the borough."

In the same year the paper printed the following little story:

"A ragged and obviously ill-nourished little boy of about eight years went into a Seacombe's grocer's shop this week and said to the assistant: 'Two ounces of ham, please. And mother said please slice it as thin as you can'.

"When the child had been served and departed an explanation of mother's request was asked for. It seemed that two ounces of ham cut thin was a regular request. Two ounces was expected to be spread over a whole family, and hence the instruction to the carver. The assistant commented it was a heart-breaking job serving in such a shop in Seacombe, where many of the customers had to make a penny do the work of a shilling..."

That little story told a lot. And so did the Chief Constable's Poor Kiddies' Clothing Fund. This was set up by the then Chief Constable, John Ormerod. Hundreds of boys and girls were issued with boots, warm jerseys and frocks. There were things called

"Poor Kiddies Outings". There was a Christmas issue of food parcels for struggling families who might otherwise have nothing to celebrate with.

A scheme initiated by Alderman John Airey was to grant allotment gardens to the unemployed which was rent-free. Over 500 plots were given out. One man said that his had been "the means of saving my reason". There were public collections for seeds, tools and fertilisers.

There was weekly visits to the pawnshops became a part of the order of things. The "pop shops" as they became to be known.

It wasn't all long, hot, happy summers and carnivals. These were long tough days of little money and little hope. Whilst New Brighton boomed with holidaymakers parts of Wallasey became a life struggle.

Children in Mersey Street, 1908. Note some of the children are barefoot.

THE SIGHTS AND SOUNDS OF THE LITTLE STREETS

There was neighbourliness in Wallasey long before community centres had been invented and 'togetherness' had become a word. Cobbled courts and terraces of little houses knew friendliness and fun as a part of their close-crowded daily life. The small streets of the old town had colour and character.
Streets in the old days were full of noise. Not traffic roar, or music cacophony, but the noise, friendly and familiar, of children playing, of hawkers' cries, and of rumbling cart wheels.
Every children's game had its own cheerful, catchy chant.
There were the calls of the coalmen, the old clothes men, and the foreign-looking salesmen who carried packs on their backs.

Gas lights hissed and spluttered on winter nights, giving off a mustard yellow glow.

On summer evenings, in Seacombe and in little alleys along Egremont and Poulton way, women gossiped on their front doorsteps, shawl-clad, and with their hair in neat buns.

In the rather more rural corners of the town, the occupiers of pretty cottages busied themselves in their big gardens. They sold mint and flowers.

In Seacombe the population was the most crowded. The families were the biggest.

In Smithy Lane, once off Borough Road (then known as Victoria Road), there was the sound of hammer hitting anvil in the busy blacksmith's shop.

There were street singers, gipsy women selling pegs and telling fortunes, and knife grinders.

There were Spanish onion men, and characters carrying great blocks of salt on their shoulders.

Children over 100 years ago played out of doors far more than children do today. Every street was a 'play-street'.

There was little traffic to bother them, and what there was mainly horse-drawn.

In areas where the streets were close together there was a hide-and-seek game called 'slippings'.

Running with hoops, guided by an iron crook or wooden stick, was a popular pastime, together with marbles ('ollies') and game called 'relieve-o'. There was hop-scotch.

Favourites among the old street entertainers were the one-man bands. Using hands to play an accordion, one foot to bang a drum on their backs, and elbows to clash cymbals, the penny-in-the-hat musicians earned every copper they got.

Of course, it was not all jolly and full of fun. There was another side.

There were children who ran the streets bare-footed. There were children with open sores and rickets.

There was, however, much to give pleasure. Sparks from the night sky from the trolley cables of the early electric trams.

The enormous sense of wealth youth felt with a penny in its pocket!

Children of over a century ago were not pampered with the latest gadgets. They got little, and knew how to make the most of it.

They made their own laughter and fun. They had within themselves the secret of delight.

Racing behind horse-drawn fire engines was a great treat. A fire, even a small one, was a real occasion.

The old engines, snorting and rumbling, had the quality of pied pipers. Children flocked after them.

Corner shops, with clanging doorbells and sawdust-covered floors, sold toffee apples and sticky sweets.

For sixpence a youngster could ruin his teeth for life.

Milkmen sold their ware from churns on little carts, pouring into jugs and basins from pint or gill ladles.

Salvation Army bands comp-pah-coom-pahed hymns and fiery evangelism. Saturday nights was their night of the week.

Brighton Street Carnival, 1920s

THE HEROES OF THE WALLASEY A.R.P

The people of the Wallasey Air Raid Precautions were the men and women who went to war in siren suits and tin hats. They were the civilian army. Ordinary people lifted out of uneventful lives and called upon to do quite extraordinary things. They came from office desks and factory bench, from shops and schools. Pensioners and housewives. They wore the proud badge of a service born in peaceful summer days in the 1930s and forged in long nights of fire and explosion and death in the blitzes of the 1940s.

It was in March, 1937, that Wallasey Town Council formed the A.R.P (Air Raid Precaution) Committee. It was an organisation designed for "the protection and well-being of the civil population in the event of war".

To many people in 1937 "the event of war" seemed only a re-

mote possibility. The Air Raid Wardens were considered a bit of a nuisance,
Then came the issue and fitting of gas masks, the census returns of shelters in the town, the formation of the Fire Guard, and the testing of sirens.
The clouds were gathering. In September, 1939, on a quiet Sunday, war was declared.
It all began with a 'false alarm'. The sirens sounded for the time on 25th June, 1940. The peak was reached during three nightmare days in March, 1941.
The blitzes on Wallasey took a total of 340 civilian lives. Over 270 people were seriously injured and 600 hurt.
The town heard over 500 alerts. The 658 high explosives dropped on it demolished 1,150 houses and damaged 17,000.
Aided by the waters of the Mersey glistering in the moonlight, the German Air Force visited the area time and again, dropping loads of incendiaries to light a beacon target for the bombers following on.
The Civil Defence was divided into groups. Each had a particular area to cover.
There were posts and headquarters. There were young messengers.
Mr. Reginald Smith was Chief Warden. His deputy was Mr. George Proudman.
There were head and deputy wardens in the various groups. There were incident officers, bomb reconnaissance officers, street fire guards, and the Home Guard.
The framework of the organisation took shape quickly. Those who belonged to it were grateful that they were introduced to ordeal by bombing in stages – never at the time appearing to be easy but subsequently judged to be nothing compared with what followed.
Soon after raids on Merseyside became general, wardens were confronted with a new problem for which little provision had been made in advance.
It concerned the use of public shelters, not only after the sirens

had sounded but for regular sleeping accommodation.

The onus of trying to create order out of chaos fell to a large extent on the warden organisation.

In group one's area was the town's largest public shelter – the basement of the Tower Building, New Brighton. The wardens were required to go there in large numbers to organise things.

In all the big shelters the wardens were responsible for the selection and appointment of shelter marshals.

Hundreds of residents sheltered under the Palace, New Brighton, in the basement of the Town Hall, in the cellars of Maris Stella Convent, and at Sandrock.

The worst raids of Wallasey's war started on the evening of 20th December, 1940. Enemy planes came over in waves.

The problem of housing and feeding the homeless was a heavy one. The Civil Defence personnel tackled it heroically.

Nights of incessant bombardment resulted in 119 fatal casualties. There was no let-up.

March, 1941, brought a long and brutal attack. Incidents were so numerous that the Civil Defence were unable to reach an accurate total for their records.

Rescue and demolition parties went sleepless, recovering the dead and the living. Fires raged about them.

Early in the attack the water supply for fire fighting failed. Victoria Central Hospital had to be evacuated owing to a breakdown in gas, water and electricity supplies.

Church Street was shattered. For a time it looked as if total evacuation would be called for. Over 170 people had been killed and 158 seriously injured. Rest centres were set up for the 10,000 homeless. Of the work of the local Civil Defence services during this period Mr. Herbert Morrison, Minister of Home Security, said: "They are an example to the whole country."

Wallasey had endured to the full the blood, toil and sweat Prime Minister Churchill had said. The facts and figures of the blitz years are recorded in the local archives ie Wallasey Reference Library, as well as log books and reports of the wardens and fire fighters.

Church Street bomb damage, March 1941

But the real story is in the memories of the men and women who were here when Wallasey learned the real meaning of total war.

Those volunteers who has been looked upon as a bit of a nuisance in the 1930s, the Civil Defence workers, were the heroes. Heroes in siren suits and tin hats.

They were ordinary men and women called upon to do quite extraordinary things and to summon up a courage they never knew they had.

They came from office desks and workshops, from store counters and school classrooms. They defended their town, their small corner of England.

They did it with guts and with cheerfulness. They did it for long dark days. They somehow managed to wear a smile, and they even found time to make music.

Wallasey was the first town in the country to form a Civil Defence Choir and Orchestra. It started in 1941, with a handful of enthusiasts and a motley collection of second-hand instruments.

The choir and orchestra gave concerts all over Merseyside. 'Messiah' and 'The Creation' in the middle of a man-made nightmare of bombs and fire and death.

They went to rehearsals tired and begrimed, picking their way through wreckage.

'Warden' was a title they were proud of. Watchmen, sentinels, of a town at war.

Though there is no monument, a grateful town have never forgotten them.

ACKNOWLEDGEMENT

Noel E Smith
Ian Roth
Percy Culverwell Brown
Edward Cuthbert Woods
Ian & Marilyn Boumphrey
T.B Maund
Martin Jenkins
Wallasey News
Wallasey Reference Library

Printed in Great Britain
by Amazon